CW00340980

Italy Unco

A Comprehensive Guide Packed with
Insider Tips to Uncover the Rich Tapestry of
Italy's Culture, Cuisine, and Spectacular
Landscape

Anita D. Brooks

TABLE OF CONTENTS

Introduction: Welcome to Italy

Overview

It is a tribute to the art of living elegantly that Italy, which is in the middle of the Mediterranean, stands as a witness. The country of Italy, which is well-known for its extensive history, cultural heritage, and delectable food, provides a broad array of experiences that capture the senses and leave an unforgettable impact on those who are lucky enough to discover its many landscapes.

The magnificence of geography

From the snow-capped peaks of the Alps in the north to the sun-drenched coastlines of the Mediterranean in the south, Italy's topography is a dazzling tapestry. The Alps are located in the northern part of the country. Over many centuries, poets, artists, and dreamers have been inspired by the attractive landscape that is created by rolling hills that are embellished with vineyards, old olive trees, and medieval towns.

Superlatives from the Past

Italy is a country that is steeped in history and so has a remarkable collection of historical wonders that span millennia. Every single cobblestone and ruin tells a narrative about the past, from the famous Colosseum in Rome, which was once the arena where gladiators fought, to the majestic relics of Pompeii, which were frozen in time by the eruption of Mount Vesuvius. Italy may be described as a living museum, were ancient civilizations and contemporary life live in perfect harmony.

Artistic Legacy

Italy is a paradise for art lovers since it is home to masterpieces that have played a significant role in the development of human creativity. The Uffizi Gallery in Florence includes works by Renaissance titans such as Leonardo da Vinci and Michelangelo, while the canals of Venice serve as a platform for the city's distinctive style of creative expression. Throughout the nation, from the Vatican Museums to the street art of Milan, Italy's cultural past is prevalent.

Culinary Extravaganza

Italian food is a celebration of tastes, a symphony of taste that differs from place to region. From the savory pasta meals of Bologna to the seafood delicacies of the Amalfi Coast, each taste is a trip through centuries of culinary heritage. Indulge in the simple pleasures of a great espresso, appreciate the richness of Tuscan olive oil, and experience the satisfaction of matching local wines with wonderful foods.

Exquisite Lifestyle

In Italy, life is not merely lived; it is relished. The notion of "la dolce vita" infuses every element of Italian life. Strolls around attractive piazzas, nighttime aperitivos, and the jubilant celebrations of local festivals all add to an excellent lifestyle that emphasizes appreciating the present.

This book encourages you to go on a trip across Italy's beauties, giving insights into each region's particular character, uncovering hidden jewels, and offering practical recommendations to make your visit easy. So, tie up your walking shoes, ready your taste senses, and prepare to be dazzled by the ageless appeal of Italy. Your quest starts today.

Why Visit Italy

Italy, with its magnetic charm, lures tourists from around the world for reasons as varied as its scenery. Here, we uncover the compelling reasons why a visit to Italy is an experience like no other.

Timeless Beauty and Architecture

Italy is a living canvas where the brushstrokes of history have created an astonishing picture. The country's architectural masterpieces, from the grandeur of the Colosseum and the Roman Forum to the ethereal beauty of Florence's Duomo and the complex design of the Leaning Tower of Pisa, tell tales of civilizations that have affected the history of mankind.

Cultural Tapestry

Immerse yourself in a cultural tapestry woven with strands of art, music, and literature. Italy has been home to some of the world's greatest artists and intellectuals, and their legacy lives on in the museums, galleries, and old libraries that dot the country. The dynamic local culture, reflected via traditional festivals, folk dances, and bustling marketplaces, presents a rich tapestry begging to be explored.

Culinary Delights

Italy's culinary landscape is nothing short of a surprise. From the simplicity of a flawlessly made pasta dish at a Roman trattoria to the explosion of flavors in a Neapolitan pizza, each mouthful is a celebration of the country's culinary history. Indulge in the variety of regional cuisines, tasting the wealth of fresh food, fragrant olive oils, and superb wines.

Picturesque Landscapes

Italy's natural beauty is an ever-changing masterpiece. The sun-kissed vineyards of Tuscany, the dramatic cliffs of the Amalfi Coast, the beautiful lakes tucked in the Alps, and the turquoise seas surrounding the islands all combine into a visual symphony that captivates and inspires. Whether you desire alpine activities, coastal peace, or rural quiet, Italy offers it all.

Hospitality and Warmth

Italian friendliness is famous, with residents greeting guests like long-lost friends. The warmth of a coffee shared at a local café, the genuine grins exchanged in crowded marketplaces, and the camaraderie felt during joyful festivals all add to an environment of inclusion that makes every tourist feel at home.

Living History

In Italy, history is not restricted to textbooks; it is a lively and alive phenomenon. The relics of ancient civilizations, the medieval elegance of walled towns, and the Renaissance brilliance in art and architecture all combine to produce a real feeling of history that envelops you at every step.

This chapter asks you to contemplate the various reasons why Italy should be on every traveler's bucket list. Each visit to Italy is not simply a voyage across geography but a soul-stirring investigation of the human experience in all its elements. Whether you're pulled by art, history, gastronomy, or the sheer beauty of the country, Italy welcomes you with open arms and offers an experience that exceeds the ordinary.

Best Time to Visit

Italy is a nation that wears its beauty in every season, yet the time of your visit may drastically affect the experiences you'll encounter. Here, we examine the finest periods to visit Italy, each giving a distinct peek into the essence of this wonderful region.

Spring: March until May

Spring marks a reawakening in Italy. The landscapes explode into color, with blooming flowers and budding trees creating a gorgeous background to your excursions. Mild temps make outdoor activities wonderful, and the shoulder season means fewer people. Wander through ancient cities, enjoy outdoor events, and eat fresh, seasonal food.

Summer: June to August

Summer is the peak season and with good reason. The sun-drenched days entice beachgoers to the Amalfi Coast, Tuscany's rolling hills beckon, and outdoor festivities spring to life. However, famous places may be crowded, and temperatures spike, particularly in southern areas.

Plan properly, appreciate the colorful environment, and indulge in cool gelato as you tour Italy under the summer heat.

Autumn: September to November

As summer says goodbye, fall ushers forth a new type of beauty. The weather stays good, and the scenery alters with warm colors. Vineyards are preparing for harvest, and it's a perfect time to visit wine areas. Crowds dwindle, allowing you more personal experiences with Italy's cultural riches. Experience the romanticism of autumn in towns like Florence and Venice.

Winter: December to February

Italy in winter is a wonderful affair, particularly in locations like the Dolomites. While northern places may encounter snowfall, southern regions enjoy cooler weather. Winter creates a calmer, more introspective environment, great for touring museums, spending pleasant nights by the fireside, and indulging in savory winter meals. Cities decked with Christmas lights offer a joyful mood.

Each season in Italy exposes a different side of its beauty, and the ideal time to visit depends on your interests and the experiences you desire. Whether you're attracted to the bustling energy of summer or the quiet beauty of winter, Italy greets you with open arms, offering a trip through time, culture, and nature.

Chapter One: Rome - The Eternal City

Explore the Iconic Colosseum and Roman Forum

Under the Shadow of Giants: The Colosseum

Imagine standing beneath the gigantic arches of the Colosseum, where the shouts of ancient crowds once resonated. This famous amphitheater, a testimony to Roman technical skill, featured gladiator battles, animal hunts, and theatrical plays. As you follow the outlines of its aged stones, consider the great spectacles that transpired beneath these holy walls. Each step resonates with the legends of emperors, and gladiators, and the pulse of a bygone period.

Immersed in Ancient Grandeur: The Roman Forum

Adjacent to the Colosseum is the Roman Forum, an archeological masterpiece that invites you to meander among the relics of a once-thriving center of Roman life. Temples, basilicas, and government buildings rise from the soil like silent sentinels, retaining the echoes of political arguments, busy marketplaces, and the pulse of everyday life. The old stones beneath bore evidence of the footsteps of Cicero, Julius Caesar, and centuries of people.

Highlights Amidst Ruins: Temples and Triumphal Arches

Amidst the extensive ruins, uncover the Arch of Titus, standing tall with its memorial of Rome's military achievements. The Temple of Saturn, with its imposing columns, alludes to the riches of the Roman Empire. The House of the Vestal Virgins, a sanctuary of holy fires maintained by priestesses, uncovers the spiritual component of everyday life in ancient Rome.

Capturing the Essence: Photography Gems

Capture the soul-stirring spirit of these historic treasures by framing the Colosseum against the canvas of the Roman sky. As the sunshine bathes the Forum's ruins in a warm glow, take the chance to immortalize the contrast of history against nature. These images become not simply photos but visual narratives of your journey through time.

After Sunset Enchantment: Nighttime Reverie

Consider returning after sunset when the Colosseum is bathed in a delicate glow, producing shadows that dance with the ghosts of the past. While the Roman Forum may sleep in darkness, the nighttime atmosphere adds a depth of romance to your journey. Under the starry Roman sky, these old stones murmur stories of triumphs and misfortunes.

Exploring the Colosseum and Roman Forum is a trek into the heart of ancient Rome. It's not about ordinary touring but about experiencing the physical history that embraces you, where each stone tells a tale, and every arch resonates with the endurance of a civilization that has made an everlasting stamp on the globe.

Discover Spiritual Wonders in Vatican City

Navigating the Sacred Enclave: St. Peter's Basilica

Crossing the Tiber River into Vatican City, you plunge into a world of spiritual and artistic majesty. St. Peter's Basilica, with its magnificent dome dominating the skyline, welcomes pilgrims and tourists alike. As you approach, the sheer magnitude of this marvel of Renaissance architecture leaves you in awe. The wide plaza in front, flanked by the colonnades constructed by Gian Lorenzo Bernini, sets the backdrop for the spiritual experience that unfolds inside.

Michelangelo's Masterpiece: The Sistine Chapel

A short walk from the cathedral brings you to the crown treasure of Vatican City—the Sistine Chapel. Entering this hallowed room, your eyes are instantly pulled upward to the heavenly paintings gracing the ceiling. Michelangelo's brush has brought to life images from Genesis, culminating in the renowned representation of the Creation of Adam. The sheer mastery of color, shape, and emotion transcends art, prompting observation and meditation.

Hidden Marvels: Vatican Museums

The Vatican Museums, a vast collection of art gathered by centuries of pontiffs, reveal a visual tale of human creation. From the ancient sculptures of the Pio-Clementino Museum to the detailed maps of the Gallery of Maps, each hallway offers treasures waiting to be uncovered. The Raphael Rooms, filled with murals by the maestro himself, look for the Renaissance atmosphere that pervades the Vatican.

Pilgrimage to the Heart: St. Peter's Square

As you depart the church, St. Peter's Square calls with its broad embrace. The tall Egyptian obelisk in its center, encircled by cherubic fountains, forms a harmonic symmetry. This piazza has seen significant events and speeches by pontiffs. Pilgrims meet here, joined in a feeling of spiritual kinship, making it not merely a place for churches but a witness to religion and human connection.

Planning Your Visit: Tips for Spiritual Exploration

To truly immerse yourself in the spiritual splendor of Vatican City, try attending a service in St. Peter's Basilica or participating in a guided tour that uncovers the rich symbolism within its architecture and artwork. Pre-book your tickets to the Vatican Museums to avoid huge queues and arrange your visit to coincide with calmer hours for a more meditative experience.

Discovering the spiritual treasures of Vatican City is not only a visit; it's a voyage into the heart of Christianity and a connection with the creative brilliance that transcends the earthly sphere. Whether you come for consolation, creative inspiration, or a connection with history, Vatican City stands as a sanctuary where the holy and the magnificent merge.

Dive into Local Life in Trendy Roman Neighborhoods

Trastevere: A Lively Tapestry of Tradition and Trend

As the sun sets over the Tiber River, go over its ancient waters to the area of Trastevere. Here, cobblestone pathways snake through a maze of old houses covered with ivy and colorful bougainvillea. Trastevere is where history and fashion mix, allowing a look into true Roman life. Join residents in lively piazzas, browse artisan stores, and relish the scent of authentic Roman food drifting from family-run trattorias.

Campo de Fiori: Markets and Nightlife Collide

A short walk from Trastevere leads you to Campo de Fiori, a vibrant plaza that morphs smoothly from a busy market by day to a frenetic center of nightlife after nightfall. During the day, visit kiosks stocked with fresh fruit, artisanal cheeses, and brilliant blossoms. As night falls, the area comes alive with a dynamic vitality.

Choose from a choice of restaurants, wine bars, and gelaterias that border the perimeter, and immerse yourself in the bustling ambiance.

Testaccio: Culinary Delights and Cultural Fusion

For a sense of Rome's gastronomic spirit, come to the Testaccio region. Historically an industrial district, Testaccio has experienced a transition into a gourmet magnet. Wander around the local market, enjoying fresh food and handcrafted items. Don't miss the opportunity to dig into the food scene, from classic Roman specialties in traditional trattorias to innovative twists in contemporary cafés. Testaccio perfectly mixes the ancient and the contemporary, producing a gastronomic tapestry that reflects Rome's developing preferences.

Hidden Gems: Neighborhood Gems Off the Beaten Path

As you tour these stylish districts, be careful to venture off the major thoroughfares. Discover hidden treasures like tucked-away wine bars, street art-adorned lanes, and charming family-owned shops. Engage with locals, relish the simplicity of a morning cappuccino, and accept the slow pace of Roman life.

Getting Around: Metro, Buses, and the Joy of Walking

Navigating Rome's neighborhoods is a treat. While the city boasts a well-connected metro and bus infrastructure, many of these chic neighborhoods are best explored on foot. Wander through little alleyways, stumble across picturesque squares, and let the serendipity of discovery lead your path. Engaging with the local beat on foot offers an intimate insight into these bustling areas.

Diving into local life in Rome's trendiest areas is an invitation to discover the city's pulse. From the timeless beauty of Trastevere to the vibrant energy of Campo de' Fiori and the gastronomic pleasures of Testaccio, each neighborhood exposes a distinct chapter in the tale of Rome. As you embrace the local pace, you become not simply a tourist but a participant in the living tapestry of Roman life.

Accommodation options

Absolutely, let's examine a selection of lodging possibilities in Rome with many suggestions for each category:

Rome's Historic Elegance: Boutique Hotels in Centro Storico

Hotel de' Ricci

Located in the center of Centro Storico.

Offers a combination of historic charm and contemporary luxury.

Walking distance to prominent sights such as the Pantheon and Piazza Navona.

G-Rough

A boutique hotel with a distinctive design in the historic center.

Each room has a chosen collection of antique and modern furniture.

Situated in Campo de' Fiori, providing convenient access to active local activity.

Trastevere's Bohemian Retreats: Guesthouses and B&Bs

Trastevere Charming House

Immersed in the bustling atmosphere of Trastevere.

Offers pleasant rooms with a combination of contemporary comforts and classic décor.

Close access to neighborhood cafés, pubs, and artisan stores

Domus Clara

A beautiful hostel in the center of Trastevere.

Provides a calm getaway with a garden for leisure.

Authentic Roman experience with customized service.

Modern Comforts: Hotels near Termini Station

Hotel Artemide

Centrally positioned near Termini Station for excellent transit access.

Modern rooms with excellent decor and facilities.

Rooftop balcony giving panoramic views of Rome.

iQ Hotel Roma

A modern hotel noted for its environmental principles.

Family-friendly with contemporary amenities and big accommodations.

Proximity to Termini Station and main attractions.

Luxury and Panoramic Views: Aventine Hill and Gianicolo

Hotel Aventino

Located on Aventine Hill, affording solitude and magnificent views.

Elegant rooms with a traditional but contemporary decor.

Close to the Orange Garden, giving a tranquil getaway.

Gran Meliá Rome Villa Agrippina

Luxury hotel with a riverbank position near Gianicolo.

Stunning views of St. Peter's Basilica and the Vatican.

Features a spa, outdoor pool, and great dining selections.

Authentic Retreats: Apartments and Vacation Rentals

Rome Unique Trastevere

A variety of lovely flats in the center of Trastevere.

Fully equipped kitchens for a home-away-from-home feel.

Personalized service and local knowledge from the hosts.

Navona Luxury Apartments

Located near Piazza Navona, providing premium holiday accommodations.

Stylish apartments with contemporary conveniences and historical charm.

Ideal for individuals seeking independence and local immersion.

Practical Considerations: Budget-Friendly Options

Hostel Alessandro Palace & Bar

Budget-friendly hostel near Termini Station.

Social environment with a vibrant bar and social areas.

Ideal for lone travelers or those on a small budget.

The Yellow

A renowned hostel noted for its colorful environment.

Offers budget-friendly dormitory-style lodgings.

Central location near Termini Station and excellent access to public transit.

Tips for Booking: Timing and Flexibility

Book in Advance for High Demand Periods: Especially during peak seasons or significant events.

Consider Last-Minute Deals: Keep an eye on last-minute bargains, particularly during off-peak months.

Flexibility with Dates: Being flexible with your trip dates might lead to additional alternatives and possibly cost savings.

These numerous lodging alternatives cater to various interests and budgets, ensuring that your stay in Rome matches with your individual travel style.

Chapter Two: Florence - Renaissance Gem

Marvel at Masterpieces in Uffizi and Accademia Galleries

Florence, the birthplace of the Renaissance, draws art fans with two prominent galleries—Uffizi Gallery and Accademia Gallery. In this chapter, we discover the riches beneath these sacred walls, where works by the greatest painters of the Renaissance await.

Uffizi Gallery: A Symphony of Renaissance Art

As you walk inside the Uffizi Gallery, you enter a place where the brilliance of the Renaissance comes alive. Rooms embellished with murals and golden frames hold works by Botticelli, Leonardo da Vinci, Raphael, and Michelangelo. Stand before Botticelli's "The Birth of Venus" and "Primavera," where myth and beauty combine, or wonder at Leonardo's cryptic "Annunciation." The Uffizi is not only a gallery; it's a symphony of creative excellence that transcends time.

Must-See Masterpieces at Uffizi:

Botticelli's "The Birth of Venus": Witness the ethereal beauty of Venus rising from the water in this renowned masterpiece.

Leonardo's "Annunciation": Explore the exquisite representation of the angel Gabriel's pronouncement to the Virgin Mary in Leonardo's early masterwork.

Raphael's "Madonna of the Goldfinch": Admire the beautiful composition and heartfelt passion in Raphael's depiction of the Madonna with the Christ Child and St. John.

Michelangelo's "Holy Family": Experience the spiritual closeness portrayed by Michelangelo in this moving image of the Holy Family.

Accademia Gallery: Michelangelo's David and More

The Accademia Gallery is home to one of the most iconic sculptures in the world—Michelangelo's David. As you approach the intimidating figure, the expertise of the sculptor becomes obvious. Beyond David, the Accademia displays a collection of Michelangelo's unfinished sculptures, affording a unique peek into the artist's creative process. The exhibit also holds works by other Florentine masters, presenting a full story of Renaissance art.

Highlights at Accademia:

Michelangelo's "David": Stand in amazement before the 17-foot marble sculpture, embodying the triumph of human spirit and creative talent.

Michelangelo's Unfinished Sculptures: Explore the intriguing "Prisoners" or "Slaves," sculptures that provide insight into Michelangelo's sculpting process and his theory of liberating humans from the stone.

Giotto's "Crucifix": Admire the emotional depth and anguish in Giotto's picture of the crucified Christ.

Sculptures by Renaissance Masters: Discover masterpieces by Andrea del Castagno, Sandro Botticelli, and others, improving your knowledge of the Florentine Renaissance.

Visiting these galleries is not only an encounter with art; it's a trek to the very heart of the Renaissance. The Uffizi and Accademia Galleries remain as living monuments to the creative talent that flowered in Florence, allowing you to experience the transforming force of human expression immortalized in eternal masterpieces.

Escape the Crowds in Boboli Gardens and Hidden Districts

While Florence's historic center captivates with its frenetic bustle, some sanctuaries give relief to the people. In this chapter, we go into the tranquil expanse of Boboli Gardens and visit secret regions where Florence's real beauty develops.

Boboli Gardens: A Verdant Retreat

Nestled behind the Pitti Palace, Boboli Gardens is a lush paradise that takes you to a world of peace. Designed in the 16th century, these gardens include rich landscapes, sculptures, fountains, and secret passageways. Marvel at the panoramic views of Florence from the amphitheater, meander into the Grotto Grande, and uncover the Isolotto— a pond filled with sculptures. Boboli Gardens is a quiet hideaway where the whispers of the past merge with the whispering foliage.

Hidden Gems in Florence: Oltrarno and Santo Spirito

Oltrarno: Artisans and Local Life

Cross the Ponte Vecchio, and you'll find yourself in Oltrarno—an area that keeps the essence of Florentine life. Wander through small lanes lined with stores, artisan workshops, and family-run trattorias. The Santo Spirito piazza is a local center, where artists make handcrafted items, and the Basilica di Santo Spirito stands as an outstanding specimen of Renaissance architecture.

Santo Spirito: Art and Ambiance

The Santo Spirito area provides a calmer side of Florence, away from the busy tourists. Explore the Piazza Santo Spirito, where a daily market unfolds, and residents meet at cafés. Visit the Basilica of Santo Spirito, constructed by Brunelleschi, to admire its architectural purity. This area emits a laid-back attitude and gives an insight into the everyday rhythm of Florentine life.

Off the Beaten Path: San Frediano and San Lorenzo

San Frediano: Bohemian Vibes

San Frediano is a bohemian area on the western bank of the Arno River. Its tiny lanes are lined with street art, antique boutiques, and eccentric cafés. The Basilica di Santa Maria del Carmine, home to the famed Brancacci Chapel paintings, is a hidden treasure. Embrace the bohemian ambiance of San Frediano as you explore artisan workshops and beautiful paintings.

San Lorenzo: Markets and History

San Lorenzo, frequently overlooked by the central market, displays its beauty. Visit the Mercato Centrale for a gourmet experience via local delicacies. Dive into the history of Florence at the Basilica di San Lorenzo and the Medici Chapels. As you explore the calmer alleyways, you'll meet artisan businesses, traditional workshops, and the vivid spirit of daily life.

Florence's attraction goes beyond its well-trodden routes. Boboli Gardens, Oltrarno, Santo Spirito, San Frediano, and San Lorenzo invite visitors who desire to escape the masses and immerse themselves in the real essence of this

Renaissance city. These secret getaways and neighborhoods give a natural counterpoint to the lively energy of Florence's busy heart.

Accommodation Options

As you arrange your trip to Florence, the appropriate lodging may boost your experience. Let's examine a selection of possibilities, each presenting a distinct view of this Renaissance city.

Historic Splendor: Boutique Hotels in Florence's Center

J.K. Place Firenze

A beautiful boutique hotel situated near Santa Maria Novella.

Blends modern style with old Florentine beauty.

Personalized service and attention to detail make it a distinctive option.

Golden Tower Hotel & Spa

Situated near the Ponte Vecchio, this boutique hotel has medieval elegance.

Offers spa amenities and well-decorated rooms.

A short walk to important attractions including the Uffizi Gallery and Palazzo Pitti.

Tranquil Retreats: Bed-and-Breakfasts in Oltrarno

B&B La Terrazza Su Boboli

Located in the Oltrarno area, giving a peaceful environment.

Features a beautiful patio with views of Boboli Gardens.

Provides a customized and private stay.

Serristori Palace Residence

A bed-and-breakfast in Santo Spirito, blending ancient elegance with contemporary comfort.

Spacious rooms and a tranquil patio for relaxing.

Close to artisan workshops and local markets.

Modern Comforts: Hotels near Florence Cathedral

Hotel Brunelleschi

Situated in the center of Florence, just away from the Cathedral.

Offers a blend of contemporary facilities and vintage charm.

The rooftop restaurant offers magnificent views of the city.

NH Collection Firenze Porta Rossa

Housed in a historic structure near the Cathedral.

Boasts a combination of contemporary design and Renaissance architecture.

Proximity to main attractions and retail centers.

Charming Apartments: Oltrarno and San Frediano

Palazzo Belfiore

A cluster of flats in San Frediano, integrating contemporary conveniences with traditional architecture.

Spacious living rooms and fully equipped kitchens.

Close to handmade retailers and small cafes.

Florence Art Apartments

Located in Oltrarno, it provides self-catering apartments with artistic flare.

Provides a unique and customized experience.

Close to Santo Spirito's bustling center and local markets.

Budget-Friendly Hostels: San Lorenzo and Beyond

Hostel Archi Rossi

A budget-friendly alternative in San Lorenzo, adjacent to the major market.

A vibrant environment with social areas and scheduled events.

Ideal for single travelers and those seeking a vibrant atmosphere.

Plus Florence

Located in Santa Maria Novella, offering budget-friendly dormitory-style rooms.

Modern amenities, including a pool and rooftop deck.

Convenient access to public transit.

Tips for Booking: Timing and Considerations

Peak Seasons: Book in advance for high-demand months, particularly during summer and large events.

Hidden Gems: Consider lodging in Oltrarno, Santo Spirito, or San Frediano for a more genuine experience.

Flexibility: Explore choices for short-term apartment rentals for a more immersive visit.

These hotel alternatives appeal to diverse interests and budgets, ensuring that your experience in Florence is complimented with the right spot to rest and recharge.

Chapter Three: Venice - City of Canals

Glide Along the Grand Canal by Gondola

Embark on a typical Venetian experience as we explore the eternal tradition of drifting over the Grand Canal in a gondola. In this chapter, we dig into the lyrical fascination of this legendary boat and the amazing sights it uncovers.

The Gondola: A Symbol of Venetian Elegance

The gondola, with its sleek black hull and intricate embellishments, serves as an emblem of Venetian luxury. Steeped in history, these handmade watercrafts were originally the major form of transit for Venetians traversing the complicated canal network. Today, the gondola remains an icon of romance and tradition, offering tourists to explore the city from a unique viewpoint.

Traversing the Grand Canal: A Venetian Rhapsody

As you board a gondola and float into the Grand Canal, you enter a world where time appears to stand still. The gondolier masterfully controls the boat, traversing the crowded river lined by old palazzos and architectural treasures. The soft lapping of water against the hull forms a melodious accompaniment to the beautiful symphony unfolding around you.

Iconic Landmarks Along the Grand Canal

Rialto Bridge: As you reach the Rialto Bridge, its elegant arches and lively market come into view. The gondola sails under this famous structure, affording a unique viewpoint of one of Venice's most recognized buildings.

Ca' d'Oro: The golden exterior of Ca' d'Oro shimmers in the sunshine, exhibiting Venetian Gothic architecture at its best. From the gondola, you can see the delicate features of this masterpiece.

Palazzo Barbarigo: Marvel at the front of Palazzo Barbarigo, embellished with magnificent statues and elaborate brickwork. The gondola provides guests with a close view of the architectural wonders that line the canal.

Accademia Bridge: Drift under the magnificent arches of the Accademia Bridge, linking the sestieri of Dorsoduro and San

Marco. The gondola ride provides a tranquil trip under this old bridge.

Romance and Tradition: The Gondola Experience

A gondola ride around the Grand Canal is more than a method of transportation; it's a trip into the essence of Venice. The gondolier, typically a storyteller as well, offers stories about the city's history and customs. The small location of the gondola makes it a great experience for couples seeking a romantic journey or anybody needing a moment of tranquility in the busy metropolis.

Practical Tips for Gondola Rides

Negotiate the fee: Agree on the fee with the gondolier before starting. Rates might vary, and bargaining guarantees openness.

Choose Scenic Routes: Opt for routes that display prominent locations like the Rialto Bridge and Ca' d'Oro for a more enjoyable experience.

Timing Matters: Sunset and early evening rides give a magnificent environment as the city lights begin to glow.

Group Gondola Rides: Consider sharing a gondola with others to cut expenses while still enjoying the experience.

Embarking on a gondola ride down the Grand Canal is a trip into the soul of Venice—a city where history, romance, and the smooth rhythm of the water mix to produce an amazing experience.

Immerse Yourself in Venetian Arts and Traditions

Venice, a city that has inspired artists and artisans for ages, presents a rich tapestry of arts and traditions. In this chapter, we dig into the colorful world of Venetian craftsmanship, the heritage of the Venetian School of Painting, and the surviving traditions that characterize the cultural identity of this wonderful city.

Venetian Mask Making: The Art of Carnival

The Venetian Carnival, a display of masks and debauchery, is a custom that goes back to the 11th century. Explore the complicated art of mask manufacturing, a skill that reached its height during the Renaissance. Visit studios like Ca' Macana or Il Canovaccio to observe artists producing masks that vary from the simple Bauta to the ornate Colombina. Embrace the spirit of Carnival by participating in mask-painting sessions, enabling you to create your Venetian masterpiece.

Venetian Glass: Murano's Artistic Legacy

Embark on a boat excursion to the island of Murano, famed for its centuries-old heritage of glassmaking. Murano's artists have made stunning glassware since the 13th century, and the island remains a hotbed of inventiveness. Visit glassblowing furnaces like Seguso or Barovier & Toso to experience the amazing process of sculpting molten glass into exquisite shapes. From delicate glass sculptures to Murano beads and chandeliers, the creativity of Murano glass is a tribute to Venice's unbroken history of workmanship.

Venetian Lace: Timeless Elegance

Journey to the island of Burano, famous for its bright buildings and the delicate skill of lacemaking. Venetian lace has adorned noblewomen and Dogs for generations, and the tradition continues to flourish. Visit the Scuola di Merletti to witness professional lacemakers producing complex designs using age-old methods. You may also get handcrafted lace as a lasting keepsake, a real piece of Venetian charm.

The Venetian School of Painting: Masterpieces and Maestros

Venice has been an inspiration for artists throughout the years, giving birth to the style of the Venetian School of Painting. The paintings of luminaries like Titian, Tintoretto, and Veronese decorate churches, palazzos, and galleries around the city. Explore the Gallerie dell'Accademia to experience the progression of Venetian art, from the Byzantine-influenced icons to the colorful paintings of the Renaissance. The Scuola Grande di San Rocco, embellished with Tintoretto's masterpieces, provides a breathtaking immersion into the Venetian creative tradition.

Venetian Cuisine: A Culinary Tradition

No tour of Venetian customs is complete without indulging in its gastronomic pleasures. Savor the delights of Venetian food at local osterias and trattorias. Try cicchetti, tiny and tasty Venetian snacks, accompanied with a glass of Prosecco. Delight in seafood delicacies like risotto al nero di sepia (cuttlefish ink risotto) or sarde in saor (sweet and sour sardines). End your gastronomic tour with a glass of Venetian wine and a dish of tiramisu, a dessert that owes its origins to the Veneto area.

Venetian Festivals: Celebrating Tradition

Participate in one of Venice's annual festivals and see the city in a colorful celebration of its cultural heritage. The Festa della Sensa, celebrated on Ascension Day, is commemorated with a symbolic marriage ceremony between Venice and the sea. The Historical Regatta in September sees a beautiful parade of vintage boats down the Grand Canal. These celebrations look into the pomp and rituals that have distinguished Venetian culture for generations.

Immerse yourself in the arts and traditions of Venice, where every mask, glass sculpture, lace design, and stroke of the paintbrush tells a narrative of a city that has been a birthplace of creativity for centuries. From the painting to the gastronomic, Venice welcomes you to witness the living legacy of its creative and cultural history.

Accommodation Options

As you plan your time in Venice, finding the proper hotel may improve your experience of this fascinating city. Explore a range of possibilities, each having its charm and viewpoint on the Venetian lifestyle.

Canal-Side Splendor: Boutique Hotels in San Marco

Ca' Sagredo Hotel

A stately hotel overlooking the Grand Canal.

Features lavish Venetian design and a private canal entrance.

Proximity to St. Mark's Basilica and the Rialto Bridge.

Palazzo Barbarigo

A boutique hotel recognized for its luxury accommodations.

Offers accommodations with views of the Grand Canal and excellent furniture.

Conveniently positioned near the Accademia Bridge and key sights.

Romantic Retreats: Charming Guesthouses in Dorsoduro

Ca' Maria Adele

A lovely hotel with beautifully designed rooms.

Nestled in the artistic area of Dorsoduro, near the Accademia Galleries.

Provides a calm hideaway with a garden overlooking the canal.

Corte dei Santi

A hidden treasure with a comfortable environment.

Located in a peaceful area of Dorsoduro, adjacent to the Peggy Guggenheim Collection.

Features a patio where visitors may unwind in the Venetian environment.

Historical Elegance: Palatial Stays in Cannaregio

Hotel Danieli

A renowned hotel with a long history.

Boasts magnificent rooms and spectacular views of the city.

Steps away from St. Mark's Square and the Doge's Palace.

Ca' d'Oro Palace Hotel

Housed in a historic palace overlooking the Grand Canal.

Offers authentic Venetian apartments and a lovely patio.

Walking distance to the Ca' d'Oro and Rialto Market.

Hidden Retreats: Apartments in Castello

Castello Charm Apartments

Stylish residences in the lesser-explored Castello quarter.

Provides a local feel with contemporary facilities.

Close to the Venetian Arsenal and the Biennale Gardens.

Ca' dell'Arco

Apartments with a historic flair near the Arsenale.

Offers self-catering alternatives and a peaceful neighborhood environment.

Within walking distance of the Naval History Museum and traditional local cuisine.

Budget-Friendly Hostels: San Polo and Santa Croce

Ostello Santa Fosca

A budget-friendly hostel in the ancient neighborhood of San Polo.

Provides dormitory-style lodgings with a sociable environment.

Conveniently situated near the Rialto Bridge and the Grand Canal.

We_Crociferi

A unique hostel located in a historic monastery in Santa Croce.

Offers a combination of heritage and affordability with contemporary comforts.

Close to the train station and convenient to main attractions.

Tips for Booking: Considerations and Insights

Canal Views: Opt for lodgings with canal views for a genuine Venetian experience.

Venetian Districts: Explore staying in various sestieri (districts) to explore distinct elements of Venice.

Local Immersion: Consider guesthouses and flats for a more immersive stay, enabling you to live like a Venetian.

These hotel options give a range of alternatives, enabling you to personalize your stay in Venice to your interests, whether you desire historical grandeur, romantic isolation, or a budget-friendly vacation.

Chapter Four: Milan - Modern Elegance

Shop in the Fashion Capital's Exclusive District

Welcome to the world-renowned fashion district of Milan, where luxury and flair meet to offer a unique shopping experience. In this chapter, we'll tour the exclusive Quadrilatero della Moda, a paradise for fashion fans seeking the newest trends from the most prominent designers.

Via Montenapoleone: The Epitome of Luxury

Begin your fashion trip on the famed Via Montenapoleone, a boulevard linked with elegance and richness. This beautiful road features flagship boutiques of prominent fashion labels, including Prada, Gucci, Chanel, and Versace. Stroll down the broad streets lined with stylish stores and marvel at the artistically embellished window displays that highlight the pinnacle of haute fashion.

Via della Spiga: Hidden Gems and Fashion Icons

Venture into the exquisite ambiance of Via della Spiga, an aristocratic street famed for its quiet elegance and hidden gems. Here, you'll meet boutique businesses boasting both known designers and developing talents. Take your time browsing the refined items, from Italian leather goods to magnificent jewelry, as you explore this renowned Milanese Street.

Via Sant'Andrea: A Showcase of Italian Elegance

Continue your fashion trip down Via Sant'Andrea, a boulevard that symbolizes Italian elegance. Discover a chosen collection of Italian and international designers, each contributing to the district's status as a worldwide fashion powerhouse. This beautiful street provides a combination of historical classics and avant-garde inventions, giving a wide palette for the discriminating shopper.

Via Manzoni: A Fusion of Art and Fashion

Complete your Quadrilatero della Moda experience on Via Manzoni, a street that perfectly integrates art, culture, and fashion. This lively road is home to premium stores, including Armani and Dolce & Gabbana. Dive into the realm of Italian fashion legends as you discover the refined offers and marvel at the combination of creative expression with haute couture.

Fashionable Tips for Shopping at the Quadrilatero della Moda

Personal Shopping Services: Many establishments provide customized shopping experiences with skilled stylists who can walk you through the current collections and aid in developing a fitted outfit.

Flagship Exclusives: Exclusive goods and limited-edition collections are typically offered in flagship shops, providing a rare chance to buy a piece that encapsulates the spirit of Milanese fashion.

Italian workmanship: Explore boutique boutiques that display Italian workmanship, from handcrafted leather products to artisanal jewelry, enabling you to take home a piece of Italy's creative legacy.

Café Culture: Take a break from shopping at the trendy cafés sprinkled around the city. Enjoy a cappuccino or a refreshing drink, basking in the trendy environment of Milan.

Evening Elegance: Experience the district's attractions in the evening when the streets are lit, and the stores emit a mesmerizing charm. Explore the stores after nightfall for a new viewpoint on Milanese splendor.

Embark on a fashion trip through the Quadrilatero della Moda, where every shop, every window, and every designer item tell a tale of Milan's outstanding contribution to the world of style. Whether you're searching for legendary fashion brands or discovering upcoming talents, this exclusive sector delivers an immersive and opulent shopping experience in the fashion center of the world.

Experience the Contemporary Arts Scene

Milan, a city at the vanguard of design and innovation, provides a lively contemporary art culture that pushes limits and challenges preconceptions. In this chapter, we'll study the contemporary art institutions, galleries, and street art that contribute to Milan's vibrant cultural scene.

Fondazione Prada: A Fusion of Art and Architecture

Embark on a cultural adventure at the Fondazione Prada, a cutting-edge institution that effortlessly melds art, architecture, and culture. Designed by famous architect Rem Koolhaas, the complex showcases a varied mix of contemporary art exhibits, installations, and performances. Explore the creative treasures inside the "Haunted House" and the remarkable architectural spaces that contain temporary and permanent exhibits.

HangarBicocca: Contemporary Art in Industrial Spaces

Immerse yourself in modern art at HangarBicocca, a former industrial area turned into a lively art venue. This enormous exhibition hall presents large-scale installations and immersive artworks by worldwide contemporary artists. Wander around the large halls and open-air regions, meeting thought-provoking pieces that expand the frontiers of creative expression.

Contemporary Art Galleries: Brera and Beyond

Stroll around the beautiful area of Brera, famed for its antique beauty and modern art galleries. Explore locations like the Galleria d'Arte Moderna di Milano, which presents Italian and worldwide modern art, and the Galleria Christian Stein, a contemporary art gallery with an emphasis on avant-garde trends. Venture beyond Brera to find hidden jewels like the Cardi Gallery, which showcases works by renowned modern painters.

Street Art in the Isola District

Experience the urban art culture in Milan's unique Isola area, where street art lends a vivid depth to the city's surroundings. Wander through the small alleyways covered with paintings, graffiti, and street installations that represent the colorful energy of Milan's current culture. Join a guided street art tour to obtain insights into the stories behind the artwork and the artists influencing the city's visual language.

Contemporary Dance and Theater: Teatro dell'Arte

For a comprehensive arts experience, attend a performance at the Teatro dell'Arte, a modern theater set inside the Triennale di Milano complex. This creative location showcases a varied spectrum of events, including contemporary dance, experimental theater, and multimedia presentations. Check the calendar for future events that guarantee to engage and challenge your creative senses.

Art in Public Spaces: Piazza Gae Aulenti

Piazza Gae Aulenti, a contemporary space in the Porta Nuova area, serves as a canvas for public art installations and sculptures. Admire the inventive artworks that complement the urban landscape, creating a dynamic interaction between architecture and modern art. The plaza becomes a center of creation, providing a unique blend of public space and creative expression.

Practical Tips for Exploring Contemporary Arts

Event Calendars: Check event calendars for Fondazione Prada, HangarBicocca, and contemporary art galleries to keep current on exhibits, performances, and special events.

Street Art Tours: Join a guided street art tour to uncover hidden street art jewels and acquire insights into Milan's urban art movement.

Museum Passes: Consider acquiring museum passes for entrance to numerous modern art locations, giving a cost-effective method to experience Milan's cultural attractions.

Nighttime Performances: Attend nighttime performances at Teatro dell'Arte for a unique experience in contemporary dance and drama against the background of Milan's futuristic cityscape.

Milan's modern art scene encourages you to experience the crossroads of creativity, innovation, and expression. Whether you find inspiration in avant-garde installations, energetic performances, or street art storytelling, Milan provides a wide and developing canvas for anyone seeking a contemporary creative trip.

Accommodation Options

Selecting the correct lodging in Milan assures a pleasant and elegant stay in this international city. Explore a range of possibilities, each delivering a distinct combination of contemporary comfort, convenience, and a touch of Milanese beauty.

Luxury Retreats: Historic Palazzos and Modern Opulence

Armani Hotel Milano

A peak of luxury situated in a palazzo in the center of Milan.

Impeccably crafted rooms embody the Armani concept.

Features a gourmet restaurant and a spa for a genuinely luxurious experience.

Bulgari Hotel Milano

A refuge of refinement located in an 18th-century Milanese mansion.

Exquisite design, a private garden, and a spa give solitude.

Located in the Brera neighborhood, it merges ancient beauty with contemporary luxury.

Contemporary Elegance: Design Hotels in Trendy Districts

ME Milan Il Duca

A design hotel with avant-garde decor in the Porta Nuova neighborhood.

Stylish accommodations, a rooftop bar with spectacular views, and contemporary conveniences.

Situated near Corso Como and Brera, it is a fashionable and handy location.

Room Mate Giulia

A boutique hotel in the center of the city, near the Galleria Vittorio Emanuele II.

Vibrant and contemporary decor, individualized service, and a handy location.

Ideal for individuals seeking a modern and dynamic setting.

Central Comfort: Hotels Near the Duomo and Shopping Districts

NH Collection Milano President

A new hotel with a clean design near the Duomo.

Comfortable accommodations, a central position, with convenient access to retail areas.

Ideal for individuals who wish to be at the heart of Milan's lively city center.

Starhotels Rosa Grand

A classy hotel located near the Duomo and La Scala.

Elegant accommodations, a rooftop patio, and an excellent location for touring.

Offers a combination of antique charm and modern comfort.

Artistic Ambiance: Hotels in the Brera District

Palazzo Parigi Hotel & Grand Spa

An exquisite hotel situated in the artistic Brera neighborhood.

Luxurious accommodations, a gorgeous garden, and a spa for relaxation.

Close to Pinacoteca di Brera and Brera Botanical Garden.

Senato Hotel Milano

A boutique hotel with a contemporary style in the Brera neighborhood.

Chic rooms, a rooftop patio, and accessibility to cultural activities.

Offers a sophisticated and cozy location for a wonderful visit.

Chic Apartments: Self-Catering Options in Navigli

Style Hotel

Contemporary residences in the fashionable Navigli area.

Fully equipped kitchens and contemporary conveniences.

Ideal for individuals who desire a more autonomous and local experience.

SuiteLowCost Navigli

Budget-friendly flats in Navigli with a contemporary style.

Convenient location for enjoying Navigli's bustling nightlife.

A wonderful alternative for individuals wanting a balance of budget and flair.

Budget-Friendly Stays: Hostels and Boutique Options

Ostello Bello Grande

A popular hostel in the city center, near the Central Station.

Vibrant environment, social activities, and budget-friendly lodgings.

Ideal for single travelers and those seeking a vibrant atmosphere.

NYX Hotel Milan

A contemporary boutique hotel with cheap prices.

Colorful and contemporary style, situated in the Isola neighborhood.

Offers a nice stay without breaking the budget.

Tips for Booking: Location and Preferences

Proximity to sites: Consider lodging near sites like the Duomo, Brera, or Porta Nuova depending on your interests.

transit Access: Choose lodging with easy access to public transit for comfortable city exploring.

Local Experience: Opt for boutique hotels, flats, or guesthouses in districts like Brera or Navigli for a more local experience.

These hotel alternatives appeal to diverse interests and budgets, enabling you to choose the right location to stay in

Milan. Whether you prefer historic luxury, modern design, or a more budget-friendly experience, Milan provides several alternatives to enrich your visit to this lively city.

Chapter Five: Tuscany - Vineyards and Villages

Savor the Flavors of Chianti Wine Country

Indulge in a sensual voyage through the lovely Chianti wine district, where the undulating hills are decorated with vineyards and old olive trees extend as far as the eye can see. In this chapter, we'll explore the rich culinary traditions of the area, from farm-to-table delicacies to the right wine pairings.

Local Markets and Culinary Delights in Greve in Chianti

Greve in Chianti Market Day

Immerse yourself in the vivid ambiance of the local market in Greve in Chianti.

Sample fresh fruit, handmade cheeses, and locally cured meats.

Engage with local farmers and producers, learning about their time-honored practices.

Tuscan Cooking Class

Join a hands-on Tuscan cooking workshop in the heart of Chianti.

Learn to cook traditional meals like ribollita, pappa al pomodoro, and homemade pasta.

Enjoy the results of your effort with a wine pairing using Chianti Classico.

Wine and Food Pairing in Radda in Chianti

Wine Tasting at Castello di Brolio

Embark on a wine-tasting excursion in the medieval Castello di Brolio.

Sample the estate's Chianti Classico and Super Tuscan wines.

Discover the art of wine matching with local cheeses and cured foods.

Dining in Radda's Osterias

Explore Radda in Chianti's lovely osterias for a genuine dining experience.

Savor regional dishes like wild boar stew, crostini with chicken liver pâté, and bistecca alla fiorentina.

Pair your meal with a glass of Chianti Classico Riserva for a real flavor of the land.

Vernaccia Wine and Tuscan Cuisine in San Gimignano

Vernaccia Wine Tasting

Delight in a Vernaccia wine-tasting session in San Gimignano.

Visit famous vineyards like Fattoria San Donato to sample the crisp white wines.

Pair Vernaccia with local pecorino cheese and bruschetta.

Dine with a View in San Gimignano

Choose a restaurant with panoramic views of San Gimignano's historic towers.

Enjoy Tuscan favorites such as pappa al pomodoro, ribollita, and handmade pici pasta.

Conclude your meal with a glass of Vin Santo and cantucci.

Olive Oil Tasting & Culinary Experiences in Montalcino

Olive Oil Tasting at Fattoria di Barbi

Experience the taste of extra virgin olive oil at Fattoria dei Barbi.

Learn about olive oil production and its relevance in Tuscan cuisine.

Sample freshly squeezed olive oil combined with local bread.

Gastronomic Tour in Montalcino

Embark on a culinary journey through Montalcino's trattorias and enotecas.

Taste the famed Pecorino di Pienza and locally made salumi.

Pair Montalcino's red wines, including Brunello, with delicious Tuscan meals.

Siena's Culinary Heritage and Timeless Eateries

Siena's Historic Eateries

Wander around Siena's medieval center and explore its timeless cafes.

Try panforte, a typical Sienese dessert packed with nuts and dried fruits.

Savor pici pasta with ragù or wild boar sauce at a trattoria off the main path.

Wine Bars in Piazza del Campo

Unwind at the wine bars around Piazza del Campo.

Enjoy a glass of Chianti Classico or Vernaccia di San Gimignano.

Pair your wine with local cured foods and crostini.

Tips for a Culinary Adventure in Chianti Wine Country

Wine & Food excursions: Consider taking guided wine and food excursions for an in-depth investigation of local tastes and culinary traditions.

Local Events: Check for local food and wine festivals, honoring the harvest season or promoting area delicacies.

Seasonal Ingredients: Embrace the seasonal wealth of Chianti by tasting recipes utilizing truffles, porcini mushrooms, and chestnuts depending on the time of year.

Culinary classes: Participate in culinary classes to strengthen your cooking abilities and discover the art of Tuscan food from local professionals.

Embark on a gastronomic tour through the Chianti wine area, where each meal offers a narrative of history, terroir, and the eternal relationship between food and the land. From the marketplaces of Greve to the lovely osterias of Radda, let the aromas of Tuscany captivate your tongue and leave lasting memories of this gourmet heaven.

Stroll Through Quaint Villages like San Gimignano

Step back in time and explore the lovely towns that beautify the Tuscan countryside. In this chapter, we'll visit the timeless appeal of San Gimignano and other charming hamlets, where medieval towers, cobblestone streets, and a feeling of history call you to slow down and absorb the beauty of rural Tuscany.

San Gimignano: Towers of Timelessness

Piazza del Duomo: The Heart of San Gimignano

Begin your visit to Piazza del Duomo, surrounded by historic architecture.

Admire the beautiful Collegiate Church of Santa Maria Assunta and its wonderful paintings.

Marvel at the majestic medieval towers that characterize the skyline of San Gimignano.

Climb the Torre Grossa for Panoramic Views

Ascend the Torre Grossa, the highest tower in San Gimignano.

Enjoy panoramic views of the town, the undulating hills, and the distant vineyards.

Capture the flavor of ancient Tuscany from this lofty vantage point.

Artisan Shops and Gelato Delights

Stroll down Via San Matteo, replete with artisan stores and boutiques.

Sample handcrafted items such as saffron-infused delights and handmade pottery.

Indulge in a scoop of gelato while walking around the lovely neighborhoods.

Monteriggioni: A Walled Haven

Circular Walls and Towering Defenses

Explore the superbly preserved walls of Monteriggioni, a medieval stronghold.

Walk around the circular walls, affording panoramic views of the surrounding landscape.

Immerse yourself in the feeling of history inside this little yet magnificent community.

Piazza Roma: Central Square Charm

Discover the quaint Piazza Roma at the center of Monteriggioni.

Relax under the shadow of the central well and absorb the ambiance of this calm plaza.

Unwind at a local café and experience the simplicity of life behind the castle walls.

Pienza: Renaissance Splendor in Val d'Orcia

Piazza Pio II: A Renaissance Masterpiece

Enter Pienza's UNESCO-listed old center via Porta al Prato.

Stand in amazement at Piazza Pio II, surrounded by the magnificent architecture of the Renaissance.

Visit the Piccolomini Palace and the Cathedral to observe the town's cultural wealth.

Cacio e Pepe Delights

Indulge in Pienza's gastronomic delicacy, cacio e pepe.

Taste the locally produced Pecorino cheese in different forms, combined with handmade pasta.

Explore the artisanal businesses selling excellent cheese and other regional pleasures.

Volterra: Etruscan Legacy and Alabaster Artistry

Etruscan Gates and Roman Theater

Enter Volterra via the old Etruscan gates, Porta all'Arco.

Explore the well-preserved Roman Theater and the Etruscan Acropolis.

Delve into the complex history that has produced this intriguing hilltop village.

Alabaster Workshops and Artisan Treasures

Wander around Volterra's small alleyways, home to various alabaster workshops.

Observe artists constructing beautiful alabaster sculptures and ornamental elements.

Acquire a piece of Volterra's creative legacy as a unique keepsake.

Charming Encounters in Certaldo Alto

Funicular Ride to Certaldo Alto

Ascend to Certaldo Alto, the historic upper town, using the lovely funicular.

Enjoy the lovely trip up the hill, flanked by olive trees and vineyards.

Step into a realm where time appears to stand still.

Via Boccaccio: A Literary Stroll

Saunter down Via Boccaccio, named for the famed author Giovanni Boccaccio.

Discover the mansion where Boccaccio resided and penned his literary masterpieces.

Relax on the calm piazzas and absorb the aura of this literary sanctuary.

Tips for Exploring Quaint Villages

Local Cuisine: Savor local delicacies in each hamlet, from Vernaccia wine in San Gimignano to Pecorino cheese in Pienza.

Historic Events: Check for any local festivals or historical reenactments that may overlap with your visit, giving a cultural layer to your experience.

Artisanal Finds: Explore the artisanal stores for unique mementos, whether it be handcrafted pottery, alabaster crafts, or local delicacies.

Off-Peak Exploration: Consider visiting these settlements during the calmer hours of the morning or late afternoon to experience a more tranquil ambiance.

Embark on a trip through the tiny towns of Tuscany, where every cobblestone has a tale to tell, and each picturesque square beckons you to remain a little longer. Whether you're attracted to the ancient towers of San Gimignano or the Renaissance elegance of Pienza, these communities give an insight into the essence of Tuscany, where history, culture, and beauty meet in perfect harmony.

Accommodation Options

Discover the ideal hideaway set within the splendor of Tuscany. From ancient palazzos to lovely country estates, this chapter features a handpicked selection of lodging alternatives that guarantee an exceptional stay in the heart of Italy's gorgeous countryside.

Luxurious Palazzos in Florence:

Villa Cora, Florence

A beautiful 19th-century home nestled amid lovely grounds.

Opulent rooms with classical décor and contemporary conveniences.

Features a rooftop patio with spectacular views of Florence.

Belmond Villa San Michele, Florence

Housed in a historic monastery with Renaissance architecture.

Elegant rooms, a gorgeous pool, and terraced gardens.

Offers a peaceful hideaway only minutes from the city core.

Romantic Retreats in Chianti:

Castello del Nero Hotel & Spa, Chianti

A perfectly renovated castle with exquisite lodgings.

Spacious accommodations, a gourmet restaurant, and a spa with wellness programs.

Surrounded by vineyards and olive trees for a lovely getaway.

Borgo Santo Pietro, Chianti

An excellent boutique hotel in a historic village.

Lavish accommodations, organic gardens, and a Michelin-starred restaurant.

Provides a private and romantic setting.

Idyllic Villas in Val d'Orcia:

Rosewood Castiglion del Bosco, Val d'Orcia

A historic estate featuring a choice of magnificent homes.

Private infinity pools, Tuscan-inspired décor, and customized service.

Surrounded by vineyards and undulating hills in the Val d'Orcia.

La Bandita Townhouse, Pienza

A lovely townhouse in the center of Pienza.

Chic rooms, a rooftop patio, and a charming library.

Offers an intimate location with convenient access to nearby attractions.

Rural Elegance in Montepulciano:

Il Borro, Tuscany

A medieval town turned luxury resort owned by the Ferragamo family.

Elegant accommodations, a vineyard, and farm-to-table dining.

Provides a combination of history, art, and Tuscan hospitality.

Conte Sestieri, Montepulciano

A beautiful guesthouse with magnificent views.

Comfortable rooms, a garden, and a terrace overlooking the Val d'Orcia.

Delivers a tranquil escape amid the Tuscan countryside.

Historic Charm in Siena:

Grand Hotel Continental Siena – Starhotels Collezione

Housed in a 17th-century palace in Siena's historic center.

Lavish rooms, frescoed ceilings, and a rooftop patio.

Offers a beautiful lodging with convenient access to Siena's sites.

NH Siena Palazzo Ravizza

An old aristocratic home with a quiet garden.

Classic rooms, vintage furniture, and a beautiful courtyard.

Combines classic charm with contemporary comfort.

Quaint Inns in San Gimignano:

La Collegiata, San Gimignano

A beautiful inn with spectacular views of the countryside.

Rustic-chic rooms, a garden, and a terrace with stunning panoramas.

Provides an intimate and genuine Tuscan experience.

Hotel Leon Bianco, San Gimignano

Located in a historic building in the center of San Gimignano.

Cozy accommodations, a rooftop patio, and a restaurant offering local food.

Offers a convenient and pleasant base for exploring the town.

Tranquil Retreats in Volterra:

Albergo Villa Nencini, Volterra

A lovely house surrounded by olive orchards.

Comfortable accommodations, a garden, and an outdoor pool.

Ideal for people seeking solitude near the picturesque town of Volterra.

Park Hotel Le Fonti, Volterra

Nestled amid the hills with spectacular views.

Modern rooms, a balcony, and an outdoor pool.

Combines a quiet environment with closeness to Volterra's attractions.

Local Charm in Certaldo:

Hotel Il Castello, Certaldo Alto

Located inside the medieval walls of Certaldo Alto.

Quaint rooms, a patio, with views of the surrounding hills.

Offers a genuine experience in this picturesque hilltop town.

Hotel Latini, Certaldo

A pleasant hotel with a combination of contemporary and rustic themes.

Well-appointed rooms, a garden, and a restaurant featuring regional specialties.

Provides a handy base for exploring Certaldo and the surrounding region.

Tips for Choosing Your Accommodation:

Location: Consider the closeness of the hotel to important attractions and whether you prefer a rural getaway or a city center stay.

Facilities: Look for facilities that correspond with your interests, whether it's a spa, pool, on-site restaurant, or historical elements.

Local Experiences: Choose lodgings that provide unique local experiences, such as wine tastings, culinary workshops, or guided tours of the surrounding region.

Seasonal Considerations: Be careful of the season you intend to visit, since Tuscany's scenery and activities fluctuate throughout the year.

Selecting the proper hotel is a crucial element of your Tuscan experience. Whether you decide for a historic palazzo, a lovely villa, or a small inn, these ideas give a varied variety of alternatives for making lasting experiences in this enchanting location.

Chapter Six: Amalfi Coast - Coastal Charms

Relax in Cliffside Marvels: Positano and Amalfi

Dive into the seaside beauty of Positano and Amalfi, where the blue waves of the Tyrrhenian Sea meet the pastel-colored cliffs. In this chapter, we'll relax in the picturesque alleys, bask on sun-soaked beaches, and discover the character that marks these great sites.

Positano's Coastal Splendor:

Spiaggia Grande: Beachside Bliss

Relax on Positano's principal beach, Spiaggia Grande.

Soak in the Mediterranean sun while gazing at the renowned cliffside houses.

Enjoy coastal attractions, from quaint cafés to exciting beach clubs.

Shopping Along Via dei Mulini

Explore the stylish boutiques and artisan stores along Via dei Mulini.

Discover handcrafted sandals, locally created pottery, and fashionable clothes.

Immerse yourself in the trendy appeal of Positano's retail scene.

Dining with a View

Indulge in a cliffside dining experience overlooking the sea.

Savor fresh seafood, classic pasta meals, and local wines.

Let the picturesque atmosphere of Positano's beach eateries enchant your senses.

Amalfi's Timeless Charms:

Amalfi's Historic Piazza Duomo

Unwind at Piazza Duomo, the heart of Amalfi's old city.

Admire the front of the Cathedral of Saint Andrew and its vivid mosaics.

Sip on a delicious limoncello while soaking in the bustling scene.

Lemon Groves and Limoncello Tasting

Explore Amalfi's famed lemon trees and orchards.

Learn about the manufacturing of limoncello, a local lemon liqueur.

Enjoy a sampling session, experiencing the spicy tastes of this Amalfi Coast delicacy.

Scenic Walks to Torre dello Ziro

Take a stroll to Torre dello Ziro, a medieval watchtower.

Revel in panoramic views of the coastline and the Gulf of Salerno.

Capture the calm of Amalfi's seaside vistas.

Cliffside Retreats and Beach Escapes:

Luxury Retreats in Positano

Check into a cliffside luxury hideaway with magnificent views.

Unwind in a private patio with a jacuzzi overlooking the sea.

Immerse yourself in the subtle elegance of Positano's top lodgings.

Charming Boutique Stays in Amalfi

Choose a small hotel nestled away amid Amalfi's medieval lanes.

Experience customized service and private atmospheres.

Enjoy the combination of contemporary comfort and seaside charm.

Seaside Adventures and Boat Excursions:

Boat Tours to Hidden Coves

Embark on a boat journey to explore quiet coves and grottoes.

Swim in the crystal-clear waters of the Tyrrhenian Sea.

Let the gentle swing of the boat improve your connection to the coastal scenery.

Hiking the Path of the Gods

Challenge yourself with a trek along the famed Sentiero degli Dei.

Marvel at spectacular views of Positano and Amalfi from lofty viewing points.

Immerse yourself in the natural marvels of the Amalfi Coast.

Capturing Moments and Sunset Serenity:

Photography Along the Coastal Walkways

Capture the breathtaking splendor of Positano and Amalfi along seaside walkways.

Frame classic vistas of cliffside houses, colorful umbrellas, and spectacular seascapes.

Create enduring memories via photography in these lovely locales.

Sunset Aperitivo on the Cliffs

Relish a sunset aperitivo from a cliffside patio.

Watch as the sun drops below the horizon, sending warm colors over the water.

Let the serene beauty of the Amalfi Coast inspire relaxation and introspection.

Tips for Cliffside Relaxation:

Beach Etiquette: Familiarize oneself with beach conventions, including the usage of designated beach areas and the availability of beach chairs and umbrellas.

Sun Protection: Pack sunscreen, hats, and sunglasses to protect yourself from the Mediterranean sun, particularly during the peak hours.

Evening Strolls: Take leisurely evening strolls around the waterfront promenades, admiring the lit cliffs and coastal environment.

Culinary Delights: Explore local cuisines by eating regional meals, seafood specialties, and refreshing sweets like sfogliatella.

Positano and Amalfi call with their seaside appeal, encouraging you to relax in the embrace of cliffside wonders. Whether you're reclining on the beaches, relishing seafood delicacies, or catching the majesty of a sunset, this chapter honors the art of leisure along the Amalfi Coast's timeless and stunning shoreline.

Explore Azure Waters and Secret Beaches

Embark on a voyage of discovery as we unearth the hidden jewels and quiet getaways situated throughout the Amalfi Coast. In this chapter, we'll journey beyond the well-trodden roads to encounter blue seas, secluded beaches, and pristine coves that epitomize the undisturbed beauty of this coastal paradise.

Hidden Coves & Tranquil Retreats:

Conca dei Marini: The Emerald Grotto

Venture into the ethereal magnificence of the Grotta dello Smeraldo.

Admire the fascinating emerald reflections formed by sunlight passing across the waves.

Explore the adjacent fishing town of Conca dei Marini for a genuine seaside experience.

Fjord of Furore: Nature's Masterpiece

Discover the hidden Fjord of Furore, a natural beauty.

Sunbathe on the little beach or enjoy a refreshing swim in the beautiful waters.

Capture the stunning splendor of the fjord, framed by towering rocks.

Off-the-Beaten-Path Beach Escapes:

Arienzo Beach: Secluded Splendor

Access the quiet Arienzo Beach via boat or a cliffside stairway.

Enjoy the tranquility of this hidden treasure, surrounded by limestone cliffs.

Indulge in fresh seafood at a seaside restaurant for a comprehensive coastal experience.

Marina di Praia: A Hidden Oasis

Explore the tucked-away Marina di Praia, a beautiful fishing town.

Relax on the pebbled beach and soak in the small setting.

Savor traditional dishes at beachfront tavernas with the sound of the sea as your soundtrack.

Azure Waters and Underwater Wonders:

Li Galli Islands: Mythical Charms

Embark on a boat tour to the Li Galli Islands, a fabled archipelago.

Snorkel in the beautiful seas, exploring undersea caverns and rich marine life.

Delve into the stories of the islands, thought to be the sirens' residence in Greek mythology.

Positano's Laurito Beach: A Serene Hideaway

Access Laurito Beach via boat or a scenic coastal route.

Revel in the quiet of this secluded refuge, surrounded by beautiful flora.

Dine at a beachside restaurant, relishing fresh seafood and local dishes.

Adventure Along the Coastal Paths:

Path of the Gods Extension: Nocelle to Praiano

Extend your trekking journey from the Path of the Gods to Nocelle and Praiano.

Traverse magnificent cliffside trails with spectacular views of the shoreline.

Immerse yourself in the natural splendor of this less-explored portion of the seaside walk.

Secret Path to Atrani's Beach

Uncover a secret road leading to Atrani's isolated beach.

Enjoy a tranquil respite with fewer people and a more intimate atmosphere.

Bask in the beauty of Atrani, one of the Amalfi Coast's best-kept secrets.

Preserving the Beauty: Sustainable Exploration Tips:

Responsible Tourism: Choose eco-friendly tour operators and support companies dedicated to sustainable operations.

Leave No Trace: Respect the natural environment by taking your rubbish with you and preventing harm to flora and animals.

Low-influence Activities: Opt for activities like hiking, snorkeling, and paddleboarding that have little influence on the coastal habitat.

Local Conservation Efforts: Learn about and donate to local conservation activities that strive to maintain the Amalfi Coast's natural beauty.

Embark on a voyage of discovery along the Amalfi Coast's secret shores, where secluded coves and virgin beaches beg you to connect with the undisturbed beauty of this coastal paradise. Whether you're snorkeling in the blue seas, finding secret trails, or enjoying the calm of remote beaches, this chapter highlights the charm of the Amalfi Coast's lesser-known wonders.

Accommodation Options

Indulge in the elegance of exceptional lodgings along the Amalfi Coast, where each stay guarantees an immersive experience among breathtaking coastline scenery.

In this chapter, we provide a handpicked selection of hotels, villas, and boutique retreats that represent the spirit of hospitality and provide a perfect hideaway for your seaside holiday.

Positano's Cliffside Retreats:

Il San Pietro di Positano

Perched on a cliff, this 5-star hotel provides breathtaking views of the Tyrrhenian Sea.

Luxurious rooms and suites, each with its patio overlooking the shore.

Indulge in excellent cuisine at the Michelin-starred Zass Restaurant.

Le Sirenuse, Positano

A classic hotel with timeless elegance and a beautiful position overlooking the harbor.

Stylish rooms furnished with vintage furniture and hand-painted tiles.

Relax by the pool, experience gastronomic delicacies at La Sponda, and appreciate Positano's charm.

Amalfi's Seaside Splendors:

Belmond Hotel Caruso, Ravello

Nestled in the hillside village of Ravello, this old mansion has unsurpassed vistas.

Lavish apartments, a cliffside infinity pool, and terraced gardens.

Immerse yourself in the calm of the Amalfi Coast.

Santa Caterina, Amalfi

A family-owned jewel overlooking the beautiful seas of the Tyrrhenian Sea.

Mediterranean-style rooms, a saltwater pool, and a private beach.

Experience true Amalfi hospitality and Michelin-starred gastronomy.

Romantic Retreats in Praiano:

Casa Angelina, Praiano

A sleek and minimalist hotel set on the cliffs of Praiano.

Stylish rooms with sea-view balconies and a trendy rooftop patio.

Enjoy the calm environment and creative flare of this boutique hideaway.

Tramonto d'Oro, Praiano

A quaint family-run hotel with a fantastic beachfront position.

Comfortable accommodations, a pool with panoramic views, and a patio overlooking Positano.

Revel in the warm welcome and authentic Italian charm.

Secluded Elegance in Furore:

Monastero Santa Rosa Hotel & Spa, Conca dei Marini

A historic monastery turned 5-star hotel, set on the cliffs of Conca dei Marini.

Luxurious accommodations, lovely grounds, and a tiered infinity pool.

Indulge in spa treatments with views of the Gulf of Salerno.

Villa Principe Giovanni, Furore

A private property with spectacular views of the Fjord of Furore.

Spacious apartments, a private pool, and terraced gardens.

Experience the tranquility and exclusivity of our cliffside refuge.

Off-the-Beaten-Path Stays:

Palazzo Avino, Ravello

A 12th-century mansion turned magnificent hotel in the center of Ravello.

Opulent rooms, a Michelin-starred restaurant, and a cliffside pool.

Immerse yourself in the splendor of Ravello's old center.

Hotel Le Agavi, Positano

A hidden hotel located on a private bay in Positano.

Mediterranean-style accommodations with sea-view patios and direct beach access.

Enjoy a calm refuge away from the busy masses.

Villa Escapes & Exclusive Stays:

Villa Tre Ville, Positano

An exquisite property complex overlooking Positano's Bay.

Private villas with spectacular views, gardens, and customized service.

Experience the ultimate of luxury and privacy.

Casa Privata, Positano

A boutique property with a fantastic position near Fornillo Beach.

Intimate rooms, a garden patio, and individualized concierge service.

Immerse yourself in the seclusion and tranquility of this beachside sanctuary.

Tips for Choosing Your Coastal Retreat:

Location: Consider the closeness of the accommodation to significant coastal towns and attractions.

Amenities: Look for options like private balconies, pools, spa facilities, and on-site restaurants.

Seasonal Considerations: Choose lodgings depending on the season, whether it's enjoying beach vistas in summer or embracing the peacefulness of the winter.

Local Experiences: Select hotels that give unique local experiences, such as cooking courses, boat trips, or guided hikes.

Each lodging along the Amalfi Coast is an entrance to a world of coastal elegance and stunning vistas. Whether you like the romantic appeal of Positano, the historical charm of Ravello, or the solitary peacefulness of Praiano, these choices provide a variety of alternatives for creating wonderful experiences on the Amalfi Coast.

Chapter Seven: Italian Cuisine Odyssey

Culinary Diversity: Regional Specialties

Embark on a gastronomic tour across the varied regions of Italy, where each locale has a distinct tapestry of tastes, ingredients, and traditional meals. In this chapter, we'll study the diverse regional delicacies that contribute to the colorful mosaic of Italian food.

Sicily: A Fusion of Mediterranean Influences

Arancini di Riso

Delight in Sicily's renowned street cuisine, arancini di riso—golden, fried rice balls stuffed with ragù, peas, and cheese.

Savor the crunchy surface that gives way to a delicious and fragrant middle.

Caponata

Experience the bright tastes of caponata, a Sicilian eggplant dish blending sweet, sour, and salty overtones.

Enjoy it as an antipasto, appreciating the combination of eggplant, tomatoes, olives, and capers.

Cassata Siciliana

Indulge in the indulgence of cassata Siciliana, a typical Sicilian cake.

Layers of sponge cake, sweet ricotta, and marzipan create a symphony of textures and flavors.

Liguria: Pesto and Seafood by the Italian Riviera

Trofie al Pesto

Relish trofie al pesto, Liguria's traditional pasta dish.

The hand-rolled pasta works nicely with the region's famed basil-based pesto sauce.

Focaccia Genovese

Treat your taste senses to the simplicity of focaccia Genovese, a Ligurian flatbread.

Savor the precise balance of olive oil, sea salt, and occasionally toppings like olives or onions.

Acciughe al Verde (Anchovies in Green Sauce)

Explore the seaside influence with acciughe al verde, anchovies served in a brilliant green sauce of parsley, garlic, and olive oil.

Emilia-Romagna: The Culinary Heart of Italy

Tagliatelle al Ragu (Bolognese Sauce)

Delight in the richness of tagliatelle al ragu, containing the legendary Bolognese sauce.

Slow cooked with a variety of meats, the sauce turns plain spaghetti into a gastronomic marvel.

Tortellini en Brodo

Warm your spirit with tortellini en brodo, little pasta packages loaded with delicious richness, served in a subtle broth.

Prosciutto di Parma with Parmigiano-Reggiano

Indulge in the delicious tastes of Prosciutto di Parma and Parmigiano-Reggiano, two recognized pillars of Emilian cuisine.

Tuscany: Rustic Elegance and Time-Honored Classics

Ribollita

Embrace the rich taste of ribollita, a Tuscan soup with bread, beans, and seasonal vegetables.

Allow the soup to boil, absorbing the flavor of Tuscan rural food.

Pappa al Pomodoro

Savor the simplicity of pappa al pomodoro, a Tuscan bread and tomato soup.

Enjoy the meal hot or at room temperature, allowing the flavors to mingle.

Bistecca alla Fiorentina

Experience the carnivorous thrill of bistecca alla fiorentina, a thick T-bone steak, skillfully cooked and seasoned.

Campania: Naples and the Essence of Southern Italian Cooking

Linguine alle Vongole

Revel in the tastes of linguine alle vongole, pasta with clams, representing the wealth of the Gulf of Naples.

The simplicity of garlic, olive oil, and parsley emphasizes the inherent sweetness of the clams.

Sfogliatella

Indulge your sweet craving with sfogliatella, a Campanian pastry comprising thin layers of dough filled with ricotta, lemon, and spices.

Limoncello

Conclude your dinner with a taste of limoncello, the lemon-infused liqueur that captures the essence of Sorrento's lemons.

Veneto: From Canals to Culinary Delights in Venice

Risotto al Nero di Seppia

Immerse yourself in the powerful tastes of risotto al nero di seppia, a Venetian dish using black cuttlefish ink.

Baccalà Mantecato

Delight in the creamy richness of baccalà mantecato, salted fish beaten into a lovely mousse.

Spread it over Venetian-style polenta for a distinctive flavor of the lagoon.

Tiramisu

Conclude your Venetian feast with tiramisu, the renowned Italian dessert of coffee-soaked ladyfingers and mascarpone.

Puglia: Culinary Gems in the Heel of Italy

Orecchiette alle Cime di Rapa

Savor the flavors of orecchiette alle cime di rapa, pasta with broccoli rabe, garlic, and chili—a Puglian classic.

Burrata and Taralli

Enjoy the richness of burrata, a fresh cheese from Puglia, combined with the crunch of taralli, classic savory cookies.

Frisella

Explore the simplicity of frisella, a Puglian bread that becomes a wonderful meal when soaked in water, drizzled with olive oil, and topped with tomatoes and herbs.

Culinary Harmony: A Symphony of Italian Flavors

Panettone and Pandoro

Celebrate the holiday season with panettone and pandoro, classic Italian Christmas pastries coming from Milan and Verona, respectively.

Granita and Brioche

Cool down with a Sicilian granita combined with a sweet brioche, a refreshing combo particularly popular in the summer months.

Amaretti and Vin Santo

Conclude your gastronomic trip with amaretti, almond biscuits, and a taste of Vin Santo, a sweet dessert wine from Tuscany.

Tips for Culinary Exploration:

Local Markets: Visit local markets to explore regional foods and connect with local merchants.

Cooking lessons: Enroll in cooking lessons to master the technique of making regional delicacies from local chefs.

Wine Pairing: Explore Italian wines that match the tastes of regional delicacies.

Seasonal foods: Embrace the use of seasonal and locally obtained foods for a genuine cooking experience.

Culinary Festivals: Plan your vacation around regional food festivals to immerse yourself in local culinary traditions.

As you travel across the many regions of Italy, let the regional specialties grab your senses, conveying stories of old customs, cultural variety, and the everlasting art of Italian food. Buon viaggio e buon appetito!

Join Pasta and Pizza Workshops for an Authentic Experience

Immerse yourself in the heart of Italian culinary traditions by participating in pasta and pizza classes. In this chapter, we'll walk you through hands-on experiences that expose the secrets of producing the ideal pasta and pizza, enabling you to bring the tastes of Italy to your own home.

Pasta Workshop: Crafting Artisanal Excellence

Introduction to Pasta-Making Techniques

Learn about the numerous pasta kinds and their geographical importance.

Explore the skill of preparing pasta dough and understanding the significance of ingredients and quantities.

Hands-On Pasta-Making Experience

Roll up your sleeves and knead the dough under the instruction of an expert pasta cook.

Discover classic pasta forms, from the simplicity of tagliatelle to the complexity of orecchiette.

Savoring Your Creations

Boil and enjoy the freshly prepared pasta, combined with genuine Italian sauces.

Gain insights into the intricacies of combining various pasta shapes with complimentary sauces.

Tips & Techniques for Perfect Pasta

Receive helpful suggestions on attaining the optimum texture, thickness, and consistency for different pasta kinds.

Explore the importance of flour, eggs, and water in generating the ideal pasta dough.

Pizza Workshop: Mastering the Art of Neapolitan Pizza

The Essence of Neapolitan Pizza

Understand the history and importance of Neapolitan pizza, a UNESCO-recognized culinary treasure.

Explore the important components, including San Marzano tomatoes, fresh mozzarella, and extra-virgin olive oil.

Dough-Making Mastery

Dive into the process of producing the finest Neapolitan pizza dough, stressing fermentation and authenticity.

Master the skill of stretching and shaping the dough to obtain the typical thin core and fluffy edges.

Sauce, Toppings, and Baking Techniques

Learn the secrets of preparing a tasty tomato sauce and choosing high-quality garnishes.

Explore the classic wood-fired oven baking method that gives Neapolitan pizza its characteristic char and taste.

Pizza Tasting Experience

Indulge in a tasting session, relishing the rewards of your effort.

Discuss the balance of tastes, the value of high-quality ingredients, and the cultural relevance of Neapolitan pizza.

Additional Tips for a Fulfilling Culinary Experience:

Local classes: Seek classes offered by local chefs or skilled craftspeople for a genuine experience.

Group Participation: Join group workshops to improve the communal and participatory components of the experience.

Culinary excursions: Combine seminars with culinary excursions to explore local markets, acquire fresh ingredients, and enhance your awareness of regional cuisines.

Diverse Pasta Shapes: Experiment with constructing different pasta forms, including regional favorites like orecchiette, cavatelli, or pappardelle.

Pizza varieties: Explore varieties of pizza, including focaccia, calzone, and regional specialties like Sicilian or Roman pizza.

Participating in pasta and pizza seminars is not only about learning methods; it's a voyage into the heart of Italian culinary tradition. These seminars provide a hands-on, sensory experience that transcends recipes, equipping you with the skills and knowledge to reproduce the beauty of true Italian pasta and pizza in your kitchen. Buon appetito!

Foodie Journeys: Culinary Tours and Local Markets

Embark on a gastronomic excursion across Italy's dynamic culinary landscape by visiting local markets and joining guided culinary tours. In this chapter, we'll explore the busy markets and guided tours that provide a sensory feast, enabling you to relish in the many tastes, scents, and traditions of Italian food.

Local Markets: A Tapestry of Flavors

Mercato di San Lorenzo, Florence

Immerse yourself in the bustling ambiance of Mercato di San Lorenzo in Florence.

Explore booths loaded with fresh fruit, handmade cheeses, cured meats, and Tuscan delicacies.

Engage with local sellers, getting insights into the native ingredients that create Tuscan cuisine.

La Pescheria Market, Catania

Dive inside the bustling La Pescheria Market in Catania, Sicily.

Witness the colorful sight of seafood vendors presenting the day's catch.

Sample local street cuisine, like arancini and fresh fish, while absorbing the market's vibrant vibe.

Rialto Market, Venice

Navigate the famous Rialto Market in Venice, a gastronomic treasure trove.

Select fresh vegetables, fish, and spices to build your Venetian-inspired dinners.

Discover the market's importance in establishing Venetian culinary traditions.

Campo de' Fiori, Rome

Stroll around the lively Campo de' Fiori market in Rome.

Indulge in the brilliant colors and fragrances of seasonal fruits, vegetables, and Italian specialties.

Learn about the significance of fresh, local ingredients in Roman cuisine.

Culinary Tours: Guided Explorations of Italian Delicacies

Bologna Food Tour

Embark on a culinary trip through the gastronomic capital of Italy, Bologna.

Visit traditional food stores, eating local favorites like as mortadella, Parmigiano-Reggiano, and Bolognese pasta.

Delve into the history of Bologna's classic foods with a trained guide.

Trastevere Food Tour, Rome

Wander around the lovely alleyways of Trastevere in Rome on a guided culinary tour.

Explore family-run trattorias and sample traditional Roman street cuisine.

Experience the warmth of Italian hospitality and the various tastes of Roman food.

Amalfi Coast Culinary Experience

Join a gastronomic excursion along the gorgeous Amalfi Coast.

Visit local markets to gather fresh ingredients for hands-on cooking sessions.

Taste regional delights, like limoncello and fresh seafood, as you tour the coastal communities.

Palermo Street Food Adventure

Immerse yourself in Palermo's street food culture on a guided trip.

Sample arancini, panelle, and cannoli from local street sellers.

Gain insights into the culinary traditions that distinguish Sicilian Street cuisine.

Tips for a Fulfilling Culinary Exploration:

Local Guides: Opt for excursions conducted by skilled local guides who can give cultural context and insider information.

Hands-On activities: Combine culinary excursions with hands-on activities, such as cooking courses or workshops.

Off-the-Beaten-Path: Seek out trips that extend beyond tourist centers to find hidden gastronomic wonders.

Wine Tasting: Choose excursions that include wine tastings to enhance your gastronomic experience with regional wines.

Seasonal Considerations: Plan your culinary travels around seasons to sample the freshest, seasonal foods.

Embarking on culinary excursions and experiencing local markets in Italy is a sensory thrill, allowing a deep dive into the heart of regional cuisines. These encounters not only tickle your taste senses but also give a cultural immersion, linking you with the culinary tradition that makes Italy a genuine paradise for food connoisseurs. Buon viaggio e buon appetito!

Chapter Eight: Activities and Adventures

Visit Must-See Landmarks Across Italy

Italy is a treasure mine of historical and architectural beauties, each monument expressing a narrative of the country's rich legacy. In this chapter, we'll walk you through must-see sites that symbolize Italy's cultural and creative past.

Colosseum, Rome

Step into ancient history at the Colosseum, an iconic emblem of Rome. Marvel at the magnificence of this amphitheater, where gladiatorial fights and public shows once enthralled the Roman Empire. Explore the Flavian Amphitheatre's majestic structure and learn about its role in ancient Roman society.

Leaning Tower of Pisa

Discover the Leaning Tower of Pisa, an architectural masterpiece and part of the Piazza dei Miracoli (Square of

Miracles) in Pisa. Ascend the tower for sweeping views of the city and marvel at its unique tilt. Explore the adjacent church and baptistery, each contributing to the spectacular ensemble of medieval Italian architecture.

Vatican City: St. Peter's Basilica and the Sistine Chapel

Immerse yourself in the spiritual and cultural splendor of Vatican City. Explore St. Peter's Basilica, a marvel of Renaissance architecture, and gaze at Michelangelo's awe-inspiring murals in the Sistine Chapel. The Vatican Museums provide a trip through centuries of art, history, and culture.

Florence Cathedral and Brunelleschi's Dome

Visit the Florence Cathedral, known as the Duomo, and marvel at the technical genius of Brunelleschi's Dome. Climb to the peak for panoramic views of Florence and the surrounding Tuscan countryside. Admire the elaborate facade and baptistery, both part of Florence's UNESCO-listed old city.

Roman Forum with Palatine Hill, Rome

Wander around the archeological treasures of the Roman Forum, the hub of ancient Rome's political and social life. Ascend Palatine Hill for a perspective of the city and discover the remnants of imperial residences. The Forum and Palatine Hill give a peek into the everyday lives of ancient Romans.

Doge's Palace and St. Mark's Basilica, Venice

Step into the luxury of Venice at the Doge's Palace, a marvel of Venetian Gothic architecture. Explore the great halls, the Bridge of Sighs, and the jail cells. Adjacent to the palace, explore St. Mark's Basilica, embellished with mosaics and Byzantine art, showing the richness and power of the Venetian Republic.

Pantheon, Rome

Experience the timeless splendor of the Pantheon, a Roman temple turned Christian church. Marvel at its spectacular dome, the world's biggest unreinforced concrete dome. Witness the movement of light via the oculus, a central aperture that links the temple with the skies.

Uffizi Gallery, Florence

Delve into the realm of art at the Uffizi Gallery in Florence. Home to an unrivaled collection of Renaissance masterpieces, including works by Botticelli, Leonardo da Vinci, and Michelangelo, the Uffizi provides a visual trip through Italy's creative growth.

Castel Sant'Angelo, Rome

Explore the history of Castel Sant'Angelo, a fortification on the banks of the Tiber River. Originally erected as a tomb for the Roman Emperor Hadrian, it eventually functioned as a papal palace and a jail. Enjoy magnificent views of Rome from its terrace.

Pompeii and Herculaneum

Step back in time to the ancient Roman settlements of Pompeii and Herculaneum, preserved by the eruption of Mount Vesuvius in 79 AD. Wander through well-preserved streets, residences, and public buildings, getting insight into everyday life under the Roman Empire.

Tips for Landmark Exploration:

Guided Tours: Consider guided tours for in-depth insights into the history and importance of each site.

Timed entrance Tickets: Purchase timed entrance tickets in advance to avoid lengthy lineups, particularly for popular attractions.

Cultural background: Familiarize yourself with the historical and cultural background of each site to increase your enjoyment.

Comfortable Footwear: Wear comfortable shoes, since visiting locations typically includes walking and climbing stairs.

Photography: Capture the beauty of these places but also take pauses to absorb the surroundings without a lens.

These must-see sites showcase the core of Italy's cultural, historical, and artistic legacy. Whether you're attracted to ancient ruins, Renaissance art, or architectural masterpieces, each site gives a unique view into Italy's fascinating history. Buon viaggio!

Experience Outdoor Adventures: Hiking, Cycling, and More

Italy's various landscapes lure outdoor enthusiasts with a plethora of adventure choices. In this chapter, we'll take you through thrilling outdoor activities, from picturesque walks to bike exploits, enabling you to immerse yourself in the natural beauty of Italy.

Cinque Terre Coastal Trail

Embark on the Cinque Terre Coastal Trail, a set of hiking routes that link the five lovely communities along the Ligurian coast. Marvel at breathtaking vistas of the Mediterranean Sea, terraced vineyards, and colorful cliffside residences. The path includes both strenuous treks and easy walks, appealing to all ability levels.

Dolomites Alta Via 1 Trek

Experience the spectacular grandeur of the Dolomites on the Alta Via 1 hike. This long-distance hiking track takes you through alpine meadows, craggy peaks, and picturesque mountain cottages. Immerse yourself in the UNESCO-listed

Dolomites, a paradise for hikers and environment enthusiasts.

Tuscany's Val d'Orcia Walking Trails

Explore the tranquil vistas of Tuscany's Val d'Orcia by trekking its walking routes. Wander through undulating hills, cypress-lined avenues, and lovely medieval towns. This area provides a calm backdrop for both short walks and lengthy excursions, enabling you to absorb the spirit of rural Tuscany.

Amalfi Coast Path of the Gods Hike

Embark on the Path of the Gods trek along the Amalfi Coast, giving magnificent views of the Tyrrhenian Sea and the coastal settlements below. Traverse old roads, view jagged cliffs, and take in the delicious aroma of Mediterranean plants. This tough climb gives breathtaking panoramas at every turn.

Cycling in Chianti's Vineyards

Pedal through the lovely surroundings of Chianti, famed for its vineyards and olive groves. Navigate meandering roads and lovely towns, exploring the heart of Tuscany by bike.

Enjoy a leisurely ride through the famed Chianti Classico wine area, with options to stop at small vineyards.

Lake Garda Windsurfing Adventure

Experience the exhilaration of windsurfing on Lake Garda, Italy's biggest lake. With its constant winds and magnificent surroundings, Lake Garda is a windsurfer's heaven. Whether you're a newbie or an expert windsurfer, the lake's different conditions appeal to all ability levels.

Via Francigena Cycling Pilgrimage

Embark on a bike trek over the Via Francigena, a historic path from Canterbury to Rome. Pedal through scenic scenery, medieval villages, and vineyard-covered slopes. This pilgrimage provides a unique combination of physical exertion, cultural experience, and spiritual meditation.

Sardinia's Supramonte Caves Exploration

Delve into the subterranean treasures of Sardinia's Supramonte area by visiting its intriguing caverns. Traverse limestone structures, stalactites, and stalagmites in caverns like Grotta di Ispinigoli and Grotta del Bue Marino. This expedition gives a fascinating glimpse into Sardinia's geological past.

Gran Paradiso National Park Wildlife Safari

Embark on a wildlife safari in Gran Paradiso National Park, home to various flora and animals, including ibex, chamois, and golden eagles. Hike through alpine meadows and deep woods, enjoying the natural grandeur of Italy's first national park.

Sicilian Sea Kayaking Expedition

Paddle around the picturesque coastline of Sicily on a sea kayaking excursion. Explore secluded coves, sea caves, and crystal-clear seas, exploring the island's unique marine ecosystems. Sicily's coastline provides a great combination of excitement and leisure.

Tips for Outdoor Adventures:

Local Guides: Consider hiring local guides for hiking or cycling activities to traverse new terrain.

Equipment Rental: If you don't have your gear, investigate possibilities for renting bikes, kayaks, or other equipment.

Weather Awareness: Check weather conditions before outside activities and prepare appropriately.

Trail Etiquette: Follow trail etiquette and respect nature to minimize environmental effects.

Fitness Level: Choose activities that match your fitness level and experience to guarantee a good experience.

Whether you're seeking the excitement of a tough walk, the freedom of cycling through vineyards, or the peace of a kayaking excursion, Italy's outdoor activities provide a broad choice of experiences for any nature lover. Buon viaggio!

Chapter Nine: Getting Around Italy

Navigating Italy's Transportation System

Italy's well-connected transportation system provides a choice of alternatives for tourists to experience the country's various landscapes, ancient cities, and picturesque towns. In this chapter, we'll take you through the subtleties of managing Italy's transportation system, guaranteeing a flawless and pleasurable trip.

Train Travel:

Italy's enormous rail network provides a dependable and efficient means to travel between cities and regions.

High-Speed Trains: Opt for high-speed trains like Frecciarossa or Italo for rapid connections between major cities.

Regional Trains: Explore smaller towns and gorgeous landscapes utilizing regional trains for a more relaxing ride.

rail Stations: Familiarize yourself with the main rail stations in each city, giving amenities including ticket offices, information desks, and baggage storage.

Buses and Coaches:

Buses are a cheap choice for visiting regions not covered by railroads, particularly in rural areas.

Inter-City Buses: Connect cities and towns effectively, giving cost-effective alternatives to railroads.

Bus Terminals: Find key bus terminals in major cities, functioning as hubs for inter-city and regional bus services.

Car Rentals:

Renting a vehicle gives freedom, particularly for visiting isolated locations and gorgeous vistas.

Car Rental Agencies: Choose from international and local automobile rental businesses, with many accessible at airports and city centers.

Driving restrictions: Familiarize yourself with Italian driving restrictions, road signs, and parking requirements.

Flights:

Regional planes enable speedy connections, particularly for accessing islands and outlying places.

Regional Airports: Utilize regional airports for flights to specialized locations, including islands like Sicily and Sardinia.

Major Airports: Navigate major airports such as Rome Fiumicino, Milan Malpensa, and Venice Marco Polo for international and domestic flights.

Ferries:

Ferries are a picturesque choice for coastal exploration and island-hopping activities.

Island Connections: Use ferries to access islands like Sicily, Sardinia, and the Amalfi Coast, enjoying gorgeous maritime trips.

Ferry Terminals: Find ferry terminals in coastal cities, offering services to adjacent islands and coastal areas.

Public Transportation in Cities:

Public transit inside cities is efficient, allowing a simple method to visit metropolitan areas.

Metro Systems: Utilize metro systems in major cities such as Rome, Milan, and Naples for rapid and easy urban travel.

Buses and Trams: Explore communities inside cities utilizing vast bus and tram networks.

City Cards: Consider city cards that give unlimited travel on public transit and provide discounts on attractions.

Walking and Cycling:

Many Italian towns are pedestrian-friendly, enabling you to explore on foot or by bicycle.

Historic areas: Wander through historic areas on foot, enjoying the local ambiance and uncovering hidden jewels.

Bike Rentals: Rent bicycles for a leisurely tour of cities with dedicated bike lanes and picturesque paths.

Planning and Booking:

Advance Bookings: Plan and arrange transportation choices in advance, particularly during high travel seasons.

Transportation applications: Use transportation applications to check timetables, order tickets, and navigate routes efficiently.

Travel Passes: Explore travel passes for trains and public transit, giving cost-effective and flexible alternatives.

Sustainable Travel:

Public Transport: Choose public transit and trains for a more sustainable travel experience with reduced carbon emissions.

Walking and Cycling: Opt for walking or cycling inside cities for an eco-friendly tour of urban regions.

Navigating Italy's transportation system is a critical component of making a memorable and satisfying vacation experience. Whether you're touring ancient cities, coastal areas, or stunning landscapes, knowing the numerous transportation alternatives can enrich your trip through the splendor of Italy. Buon viaggio!

Efficient Use of Trains, Buses, and Metros

Efficiently managing Italy's public transportation system may improve your trip experience and enable you to tour the country easily. In this chapter, we'll coach you on the optimal use of trains, buses, and metros, guaranteeing seamless travel throughout cities and regions.

Trains:

High-Speed Trains:

Utilize high-speed trains like Frecciarossa and Italo for rapid connections between major cities.

Book tickets in advance to receive reduced costs and assure availability, particularly during popular travel seasons.

Regional Trains:

Explore tiny towns and picturesque routes utilizing regional trains.

Check the train timetable and frequency, since regional trains may have fewer frequent departures.

Train Stations:

Familiarize yourself with significant rail stations in each city, such as Termini in Rome or Milano Centrale in Milan.

Use station services including information desks, baggage storage, and rest places.

Rail Passes:

Consider train passes for cost-effective travel if you want to see many locations within a specified period.

Check the terms and restrictions of train passes to ensure they fit your trip schedule.

Buses:

Inter-City Buses:

Research and pick trustworthy bus operators for inter-city travel.

Book bus tickets in advance, particularly for popular routes or during high travel seasons.

Regional Buses:

Check regional bus timetables for trips to smaller towns or rural regions.

Be aware of any special bus terminals or stations in each city.

Airport Shuttles:

Use airport shuttle services for easy transportation between airports and city centers.

Check the timetable and pick-up/drop-off places for airport shuttles.

Metros:

Metro Systems:

Learn the metro systems in big cities including Rome, Milan, and Naples.

Purchase metro tickets or travel cards for simple access to metro services.

Metro Etiquette:

Respect metro etiquette, such as letting people depart before boarding and giving up seats to those in need.

Be mindful of peak hours when metro services may be packed.

Connections to Landmarks:

Identify metro stations that link to major monuments and attractions.

Use metro maps to create effective itineraries that minimize transfers.

Planning Your Journey:

Transportation Apps:

Download transportation applications to monitor real-time timetables, routes, and delays.

Use apps for ticket reservations and electronic boarding passes if available.

Multi-City Passes:

Explore multi-city passes that give packaged transit alternatives for trains, buses, and metros.

Evaluate the coverage and cost-effectiveness of multi-city passes.

Combining Modes of Transport:

Combine several forms of transit for efficient travel. For example, employ a high-speed rail for long-distance travel and buses or metros for local exploration.

Consider walking or cycling for short distances inside cities.

Sustainable Travel:

Public Transport Choices:

Opt for public transportation choices to lessen your carbon impact.

Choose trains, buses, and metros over private vehicle rentals for more ecologically responsible travel.

Walking and Cycling:

Embrace walking and cycling for short distances inside cities, contributing to a sustainable travel experience.

Efficiently utilizing trains, buses, and metros in Italy helps you to optimize your time, explore the local culture, and travel the nation with ease. With careful preparation, a modicum of experience with transit systems, and the use of contemporary technologies, you'll find yourself smoothly.

enjoying the stunning landscapes and dynamic towns of Italy. Buon viaggio!

Renting Cars and Exploring at Your Pace

Renting a vehicle in Italy offers up a world of options, enabling you to explore the country at your leisure and wander off the usual route. In this chapter, we'll take you through the process of hiring automobiles and give recommendations for a fun and flexible road trip experience.

Renting a Car:

Car Rental Agencies:

Choose from well-known worldwide vehicle rental firms such as Hertz, Avis, and Europcar, as well as trustworthy local ones.

Compare costs and read reviews to find a dependable rental service.

Booking in Advance:

Secure your rental vehicle by reserving, particularly during high travel seasons.

Take advantage of internet platforms and discounts for the finest bargains.

Types of Cars:

Consider the size and style of automobile that meets your trip requirements. Compact automobiles are appropriate for urban travel, whereas SUVs may be selected for rural trips.

Driving in Italy:

Driving Regulations:

Familiarize yourself with Italian driving legislation, road signs, and speed restrictions.

Carry your driver's license, passport, and rental vehicle paperwork always.

ZTL Zones:

Be wary of Zona a Traffico Limitato (ZTL) zones in ancient city centers, where only approved cars are permitted.

Research and observe local driving regulations to avoid penalties.

Parking:

Locate secure parking spots, particularly in city centers where street parking may be scarce.

Utilize paid parking facilities for peace of mind.

Scenic Routes and Itineraries:

Coastal Roads:

Explore Italy's magnificent coastline routes, such as the Amalfi Coast or the Cinque Terre, for spectacular vistas of the Mediterranean.

Take your time to stop at picturesque overlooks and attractive seaside communities.

Countryside Routes:

Venture into the lovely countryside of Tuscany or Umbria, enjoying the undulating hills, vineyards, and old towns.

Plan your trip to cover lesser-known treasures and local sights.

Mountainous Regions:

Drive across the picturesque alpine areas of the Dolomites or the Italian Alps for panoramic vistas.

Check road conditions, particularly during winter months, and be prepared for high terrain.

GPS and Navigation:

GPS Navigation:

Use a GPS gadget or navigation application on your smartphone for convenient route planning.

Download offline maps to traverse places with low network connectivity.

Road Signs:

Pay attention to traffic signage, particularly while going through cities and rural regions.

Follow directing markers to renowned tourist spots.

Fuel and Service Stations:

Fueling Up:

Locate gas stations along your trip and top up your tank before beginning on longer excursions.

Check whether your rental automobile needs diesel or petrol.

Service Stations:

Be wary of service stations giving bathrooms, food, and necessities.

Plan pauses throughout lengthy travels to keep refreshed and enjoy local food.

Local Experiences:

Off-the-Beaten-Path Stops:

Discover hidden jewels and off-the-beaten-path stops by taking unplanned diversions.

Engage with locals and ask for suggestions for real experiences.

Local Cuisine:

Explore local gastronomic pleasures in tiny towns and villages.

Taste regional delicacies and eat at family-run enterprises for a genuine experience.

Safety and Precautions:

Emergency Contacts:

Save emergency contacts, including local emergency agencies and your rental vehicle provider's hotline.

Familiarize oneself with the European emergency number, 112.

Insurance Coverage:

Understand your rental automobile insurance coverage, including liability, collision damage waiver (CDW), and theft protection.

Consider extra insurance choices for peace of mind.

Renting a vehicle in Italy allows the opportunity to construct your schedule, discover hidden jewels, and immerse yourself in the splendor of the nation. By following these recommendations and embracing the spontaneity of the open road, you'll go on a road trip journey that enables you to thoroughly appreciate the different landscapes and rich culture of Italy. Buon viaggio!

Coastal Ferries and Water Taxis for Scenic Commutes

Italy's coastal districts offer not just breathtaking vistas but also the option for pleasant commutes on coastal ferries and water taxis. In this chapter, we'll lead you through the experience of traveling by sea, including recommendations for appreciating the beauty of Italy's beaches from the water.

Coastal Ferries:

Connecting Islands and Mainland:

Utilize coastal ferries to link mainland towns with picturesque islands such as Sicily, Sardinia, and the Aeolian Islands.

Check boat timetables in advance, particularly during high travel seasons.

Breathtaking Views:

Enjoy breathtaking views of the coastline and the open sea throughout your boat voyage.

Opt for outdoor seats to truly immerse yourself in the beautiful beauty.

Ferry Routes:

Research the various ferry routes to organize your seaside commute properly.

Consider paths that give the most stunning vistas and access to hidden jewels.

Water Taxis:

City Water Transport:

Experience the pleasure of city water transit in locations like Venice, where water taxis cruise the gorgeous canals.

Pre-book water taxis for easy transfers, particularly from airports to city centers.

Exploring Coastal Cities:

Use water taxis to visit coastal communities with waterfront attractions.

Discover secluded coves, ancient ports, and thriving waterfront neighborhoods.

Scenic Transfers:

Choose water taxis for trips between coastal regions for a unique and picturesque commute.

Enjoy the simplicity of direct point-to-point transportation with the additional pleasure of seaside vistas.

Island-Hopping Adventures:

Exploring Archipelagos:

Embark on island-hopping experiences in locations with archipelagos, such as the Amalfi Coast and the Tuscan Archipelago.

Plan your plan to visit different islands and discover their distinct beauty.

Remote Coastal Villages:

Discover distant coastal settlements accessible by boat, affording a real peek into local life.

Explore less-visited areas with distinct cultural and natural features.

Tips for Scenic Sea Journeys:

Booking in Advance:

Secure your ferry or water taxi tickets in advance, particularly during high-demand months.

Check for any discounts or package packages for numerous travels.

Outdoor Seating:

Opt for outdoor seats on boats to completely experience the seaside vistas and snap unforgettable images.

Bring sunscreen and sunglasses for comfort on maritime voyages.

Local Recommendations:

Seek advice from locals or boat operators for the most picturesque routes and hidden jewels.

Inquire about any seasonal events or festivals celebrated near the shore.

Sustainable Sea Travel:

Eco-Friendly Choices:

Choose ferry companies and water taxi services devoted to eco-friendly operations.

Support sustainable marine transport choices that emphasize environmental protection.

Reducing Plastic Waste:

Bring a reusable water bottle and food to decrease plastic waste on marine travels.

Dispose of rubbish appropriately and participate in any recycling activities aboard.

Embarking on coastal ferries and water taxis in Italy gives a unique view of the country's various landscapes. Whether you're viewing the Amalfi Coast from the deck of a boat or floating through the canals of Venice in a water taxi, these gorgeous journeys offer an added layer of magic to your Italian holiday. Buon viaggio!

Chapter Ten: Practical Tips for Visitors

Learn Basic Italian Phrases and Cultural Etiquette

Immerse yourself in the rich cultural fabric of Italy by learning some basic Italian phrases and understanding cultural etiquette. In this chapter, we'll provide you with crucial language skills and cultural insights to improve your interactions and experiences while seeing the lovely nation.

Essential Italian Phrases:

Greetings:

Buongiorno: Good morning.

Buonasera: Good evening.

Ciao: Hello/goodbye (informal).

Polite Expressions:

Per favore: Please.

Grazie: Thank you.

Prego: You're welcome.

Basic Conversations:

Come stai?: How are you?

Mi chiamo...: My name is...

Posso avere il conto?: Can I have the bill?

Navigating Places:

Dove si trova...?: Where is...?

Stazione: Train station.

Bagno: Bathroom.

Food & Dining:

Menu: Menu.

Acqua: Water.

Vino: Wine.

Numbers:

Uno: One.

Due: Two.

Dieci: Ten.

Cultural Etiquette:

Greetings and Farewells:

When visiting businesses or small institutions, it's usual to greet the owner or personnel with a cheerful "buongiorno" or "buonasera."

A handshake is a frequent greeting in official contexts, whereas friends and relatives may exchange cheek kisses.

Dress Modestly at Religious Sites:

When visiting churches and religious locations, dress modestly by covering shoulders and knees.

Avoid wearing beachwear or exposing attire in places of worship.

Take Your Time When Dining:

Italians love a leisurely eating experience, so don't hurry through meals.

It's normal to linger over coffee and chat after dinner.

Show Respect in Museums and Historical Sites:

Follow norms and restrictions while visiting museums and historical places.

Avoid touching artworks and artifacts unless specifically authorized.

Expressing Appreciation for Food:

Italians take pride in their food, thus expressing satisfaction with a meal is valued.

A simple "Buonissimo!" (Very excellent) or "Delizioso!" (scrumptious) communicates your enthusiasm.

Small Talk Matters:

Italians typically indulge in light conversation before getting down to business.

Don't be startled if talks go into personal matters, since creating rapport is crucial.

Language Learning Resources:

Language Apps:

Duolingo, Babbel, and Rosetta Stone are good language-learning applications for beginners.

Use flashcards and repetition to reinforce new language.

Online Courses:

Explore online language classes provided by sites like Coursera or local language institutions.

Join language exchange programs to practice with native speakers.

Phrasebooks:

Carry a pocket-sized Italian phrasebook for fast reference throughout your travels.

Many travel guidebooks also feature basic language sections.

By adopting these fundamental Italian words and cultural etiquette suggestions into your travel toolbox, you'll not only explore Italy with greater comfort but also connect more genuinely with the people. Embrace the language and culture, and you'll find your Italian adventure enhanced by the warmth of true cultural interchange. Buona fortuna (good luck) in your language journey!

Stay Safe with Health Tips and Emergency Contacts

Ensuring your health and safety is a primary consideration when experiencing Italy. In this chapter, we'll share vital health guidelines and emergency contacts to help you remain well-prepared during your travel.

Health Tips:

Travel Insurance:

Obtain comprehensive travel insurance that covers medical emergencies, trip cancellations, and unforeseen catastrophes.

Confirm coverage for any pre-existing medical problems.

Health Precautions:

Check whether any vaccines or health precautions are advised before flying to Italy.

Carry a basic first aid kit with necessities like bandages, pain relievers, and any personal prescriptions.

Stay Hydrated:

Italy's temperature may be scorching, particularly in the summer, so remain hydrated by drinking lots of water.

Always carry a reusable water bottle and refill it during the day.

Sun Protection:

Protect yourself from the sun by wearing sunscreen, sunglasses, and a hat.

Seek cover during peak sunshine hours to minimize heat-related illnesses.

Local Pharmacies:

Familiarize yourself with the location of local pharmacies (Pharmacia) in the locations you'll be visiting.

Pharmacists in Italy may give help for mild illnesses.

Emergency Contacts:

Emergency Number:

Dial 112 for emergencies, the global emergency number in Italy.

The operator will link you to the relevant agencies, such as police, medical aid, or fire rescue.

Medical Assistance:

For medical emergencies, phone 118 to access emergency medical services (Pronto Soccorso).

Be prepared to disclose your location, specifics of the incident, and any required information about the individual in need of aid.

Police Assistance:

In case of any criminal or safety concerns, call the police by phoning 113.

Report thefts or emergencies quickly to the local police station (Questura).

Fire Emergency:

For fire situations, phone 115 to contact the fire department (Vigili del Fuoco).

Provide precise information about the location and nature of the situation.

Consular Assistance:

Locate the closest embassy or consulate of your native country for diplomatic help.

Keep the contact information, especially after-hours emergency numbers, readily accessible.

General Safety Tips:

Secure Your Belongings:

Be attentive in busy situations and safeguard your possessions to avoid theft.

Use anti-theft measures such as money belts or secret pouches.

Stay Informed:

Stay updated about local news and any travel warnings.

Follow the advice of local authorities and alter your preparations appropriately.

Emergency Translation Tools:

Have a translation software or phrasebook ready to relay basic emergency information.

Ensure vital health information may be given in Italian if required.

Register with Your Embassy:

Register with your embassy or consulate upon arrival, giving information about your stay.

This improves communication in case of crises or natural catastrophes.

By prioritizing your health, remaining informed, and knowing the emergency contacts, you may comfortably tour Italy with an emphasis on safety and well-being. Remember to alter these guidelines depending on your health requirements and the geographical places you intend to visit. Buon viaggio! (Safe travels!)

Pack Smart: What to Bring and Essential Travel Gear

Packing effectively is vital for a smooth and comfortable vacation to Italy. In this chapter, we'll advise you on what to carry and propose necessary travel goods to increase your comfort and convenience throughout your Italian vacation.

Clothing:

Weather-Appropriate Attire:

Pack clothes suited for the season and area weather. Summers may be warm, but winters vary by area.

Include suitable walking shoes for touring historic buildings and cobblestone streets.

Modest Attire for Religious Sites:

Bring modest attire, covering shoulders and knees, for trips to churches and religious places.

A light scarf or shawl might be beneficial for covering shoulders.

Smart Casual for Dining:

Pack good casual wear for eating out, particularly in upmarket establishments.

Italians frequently dress nicely, so consider somewhat formal wear for nights out.

Swimwear:

If you want to visit coastal locations or hotels with pools, take a swimsuit.

A lightweight and quick-drying travel towel might be beneficial.

Travel Essentials:

Documents and Identification:

Carry your passport, travel insurance paperwork, and any applicable visas.

Make photocopies of crucial papers and preserve them separately.

Travel Wallet:

Use a safe travel wallet to manage coins, credit cards, and other papers.

RFID-blocking wallets may assist in guarding against electronic theft.

Adapters and Chargers:

Bring universal travel adapters to charge your electrical gadgets.

Consider a portable charger for on-the-go power.

Language Resources:

Carry a pocket-sized Italian phrasebook or download language apps for easy reference.

Language translation technologies may aid in communicating.

Technology:

Smartphone and Apps:

Use your smartphone for navigation, translation, and photos.

Download vital travel applications for transportation, language, and cultural insights.

Camera:

Pack a tiny camera or use your smartphone to record great moments.

Consider a lightweight and flexible camera for photography enthusiasts.

E-Reader or Tablet:

Bring an e-reader or iPad for amusement during travel or downtime.

Load it with e-books, travel guides, and offline maps.

Health and Safety:

Basic First Aid Kit:

Assemble a basic first aid kit containing bandages, painkillers, and other essential drugs.

Include motion sickness medications if you want to enjoy scenic drives.

Personal Care Items:

Pack personal care essentials such as toothbrushes, toothpaste, and any particular toiletries.

Sunscreen and bug repellent are vital, particularly in warmer months.

Reusable Water Bottle:

Stay hydrated by carrying a reusable water bottle.

Collapsible bottles save space when not in use.

Luggage and Organization:

Suitcase or Backpack:

Choose baggage that matches your travel style—whether a suitcase with wheels or a backpack.

Consider the size and weight constraints for planes and transit.

Packing Cubes:

Use packing cubes to arrange clothes and accessories inside your suitcase.

Compression packs may conserve room for bulkier objects.

Daypack or Crossbody Bag:

Bring a tiny daypack or crossbody bag for everyday outings.

Ensure its secure to discourage pickpockets.

Miscellaneous:

Sunglasses and Hat:

Protect yourself from the sun with sunglasses and a hat.

A wide-brimmed hat gives extra shade.

Travel Umbrella:

A tiny and lightweight travel umbrella might be beneficial in case of unexpected rain.

Check the weather prediction and prepare appropriately.

Travel Journal:

Capture your adventures by taking a travel diary or notepad.

Documenting your travel gives a personal touch to your experience.

Sustainability:

Reusable Shopping Bag:

Carry a folding, reusable shopping bag for purchases and to prevent plastic waste.

Many cities in Italy restrict the usage of plastic bags.

Reusable Cutlery and Water Filter:

Consider taking reusable cutlery and a water filter for eco-friendly eating.

Reduce single-use plastic use throughout your vacation.

By following these packing suggestions and choosing the necessary travel items, you'll be well-prepared to tour Italy comfortably and quickly. Tailor your packing list based on your unique schedule, activities, and personal preferences, guaranteeing a smooth and comfortable travel. Buon viaggio! (Safe travels!)